BEGINNING
RACQUETBALL

Andy Kozar

and

Emile Catignani

*The University of Tennessee
Knoxville*

Hunter Textbooks Inc.

Printed in the United States of America.

©1997 by Hunter Textbooks Inc.

ISBN 0-88725-236-2

Inquiries should be addressed to:

ᕼᓵ Hunter Textbooks Inc.

823 Reynolda Road
Winston-Salem, North Carolina 27104

Acknowledgements

These authors needed and received assistance from a number of talented people in completing this project. We are deeply indebted to each of them for their important contributions to the preparation of *Beginning Racquetball.*

The three people, all University of Tennessee staff members, that deserve our special thanks are listed below with a brief mention of their specific contributions. They were lavish with their talent, time and insights. Without them this book could never have been properly completed.

Ernest Robertson Jr., executive director of the UT Photographic Center, used his extensive skills and lengthy experience of photographing sporting events to shoot and advise on the still photographs and sixty-four frames per second 16mm racquetball sequences used for drawings in this edition.

Hugh Bailey, a talented artist and graphics art designer, graciously gave hours of his personal time creating the line drawings and computer-generated diagrams that are so essential in supporting the written descriptions of racquetball play.

Kathryn Aycock, a professional editor, donated her free time and her considerable editorial abilities to bear on the authors basic copy.

Finally, the authors wish to make it clear that they take full responsibility for any errors in this book and they will endeavor to make every effort to correct these in future editions.

Preface

In the mid 1950s, as a graduate student at the University of Michigan, I was introduced to the four-wall game of paddleball. Not long after that I met Michigan's Earl Riskey, the man who originated the four-wall game in 1930. He became my teacher, instilling a love for the four-wall paddle game and squash racquets that has stayed with me for more than thirty-five years. Paddleball grew in popularity getting its greatest boost as an activity used in the United States Armed Forces conditioning programs on the Mid-west university campuses in the early 1940s. It was carried to other areas of the country by Riskey's students who taught by word-of-mouth, since there was little written material available on the game. In the year prior to moving to Tennessee I talked Riskey and my doubles partner, Rod Grambeau, into collaborating with me on writing a paddleball book which was published in 1967 in the popular Wadsworth Publishing Companies' sport skills series.

After the book was published we traveled to Chicago to ask the president of the United States Handball Association, the late Robert W. Kendler, to support and promote paddleball through his very popular handball magazine, *ACE*. He did this, but the agreement was short lived. In my judgment, the main reason was Joe Sobek's game of racquetball, founded in 1949. This new game began to invade handball courts, providing participants with a new, exciting faster-paced game. Kendler's interest in the game must have begun with his discovery that the game of racquetball had no formal organization or leadership. In short, the game captured his interest, imagination and business mind. He provided outstanding leadership and promotional skills for the game of racquetball that ensured its success. Since then, handball courts have been filled with people of all ages playing the new game. As a matter of fact handball courts in established facilities were renamed racquetball courts, and this was followed by a phenomenal building program of racquetball clubs.

Like almost everyone else who had access to four-wall courts, I picked up a racquet, played, and later taught racquetball, although I never gave up playing and teaching paddleball and squash racquets. These three games are more alike than they are different. Great paddleball and squash racquet players have a history of excelling in racquetball competition at both the amateur and professional levels of play.

Over the years I've taught a physical education majors' class the four-wall "wrist" games based on the three games, racquetball, paddleball and squash racquets, emphasizing their similarities and differences. Two of my better students in the "wrist" games were my co-author, Emile Catignani, and Davey Bledsoe. Davey, highly skilled and motivated went on to play racquetball professionally, eventually winning the World Professional Singles Champion-ship. Emile, a fine player with excellent technique, is enjoying a very success-ful career as an amateur player and teacher of racquetball at The University of Tennessee. As an undergraduate Emile was instrumental in The University of Tennessee's only intercollegiate national championship team and since joining our teaching staff has taught thousands of beginning players the game of racquetball.

Beginning Racquetball is a product of —

- years of experience in teaching and playing four-wall games, especially racquetball.

- a critical review of existing introductory texts on racquetball, many of which are filled with sentimentality about the game, blatant commercials for equipment, sports/racquetball jargon, and careless optimism on how well the beginner will perform as a result of using their particular book.

- a belief that there is a need for a simple, direct treatment in written form of the basic elements essential in the education of a beginning racquetball player to complement the instructors work with the students.

This book has been prepared for the student as enrichment material for beginning racquetball and as a supplement to lessons taught by a competent instructor in an organized educational setting. Therefore, such issues as stretching, injury care, complex strategy, physical conditioning, and related matters are left entirely to the discretion of the instructor of the class. Which of these and how much is needed by individuals in the class is best determined by the instructor.

No sentimentality or special claims have been made about the mental or physical value of learning to play racquetball except it can be fun to play. Most students can improve their game at a variety of skill levels through quality instruction depending on their innate physical ability, desire to improve, and willingness to work hard on improving their skills and strategy through practice and play. Hence, no careless optimism is expressed in this book as to how well one will be able to perform any aspect of the game by just using this book.

Beginning players can improve their performance with little effort at first. Significant progress will come about with good individual instruction including constant criticism of technique. In addition to good instruction, further improvement in playing the game depends on the students efforts to carefully study, understand and practice the basics as taught by the instructor and covered in this book.

Finally, when reading this book one must remember that **to simplify the text the authors assume that the performer and opponents are right handed.**

Andy Kozar

Illustrations

TABLE OF CONTENTS

BEFORE YOU BEGIN

■ Brief History

Racquetball owes its origins to the Irish game of handball and the American game of paddleball. It is played on a twenty-by-forty-by-twenty foot court originally designed for handball. The basic rules for all three games are virtually the same.

The game of racquetball was devised in 1949 by Joe Sobek of Greenwich, Connecticut. After playing and observing the game of paddleball over a period of time, Sobek believed the game could be made more interesting by increasing its pace. He substituted a strung racquet for the plywood paddle and introduced a livelier ball. Racquetball didn't gain in popularity at first, but when it did in the late 1960s and early 1970s, several governing organizations competed for control of the game.

The International Racquetball Association (I.R.A.) and the United States Racquetball Association (U.S.R.A.) both sought to govern the amateur and professional levels of the sport during the early seventies. After fostering the growth of professional racquetball, the U.S.R.A. eventually ceased to exist . Meanwhile, the I.R.A. concentrated its efforts toward the amateur game and eventually became the American Amateur Racquetball Association (A.A.R.A). The A.A.R.A. is recognized by the United States Olympic Committee as the official ruling body in racquetball. Today, racquetball is one of the more popular court games in the United States. It is an activity that appeals to all ages and is taught and played at most colleges and universities that have handball courts, which are now called racquetball courts in most places. At the 1984 Olympic Games racquetball was chosen as one of the exhibition sports, providing increased international exposure for the sport.

■ The Ball

The ball used in racquetball has evolved from being pressurized (fabricated as a closed sphere with higher than normal internal air pressure as is done in the construction of a tennis ball) to being pressureless (a ball constructed under normal internal atmospheric air pressure). This development is important because the present day ball owes its liveliness to the quality of the rubber used in its

Figure 1.1. Racquetball, racquet, and lensed eye protection

fabrication as opposed to increased internal air pressure. With this development, the durability of the ball has been greatly improved.

The official racquetball rules specify that the game ball "at a room temperature of 70–74 degrees Fahrenheit, should rebound 68–72 inches from a drop of 100 inches." Therefore, a ball that will rebound from the court floor to approximately eye level from a drop as high as one can reach would meet the specified rules. Even though various brand named racquetballs are recognized by the A.A.R.A. as "official" balls for tournament play, any racquetball can be used in practice and recreational play. Racquetballs are manufactured in several colors with blue being the most popular.

■ The Racquet

The racquet has undergone many changes since the game's inception. It evolved from little more than what appeared to be a sawed-off wooden tennis racquet (at one time labeled "paddle racquet" on the throat) to being constructed from a variety of sturdy new materials such as boron, graphite, and ceramics. Shapes and sizes of racquet frames vary, and differing string patterns are used. Rules for the game, once restrictive regarding racquet frame shapes and sizes, have since been modified to accommodate the new racquet models with larger striking surfaces.

The important factors a beginning player should consider when purchasing a racquet are grip size, weight, racquet frame size, and overall length. The circumference of the grip should be small enough that the hand can be placed around the handle with the two middle fingers of the hand nearly contacting the thick part of the thumb (see Figure 1.2). The weight of the racquets differ. If the weight is not marked on the racquet, search for one that has the weight indicated and compare the relative weight of the two before selecting one for personal use. The extra power and reach made possible by the

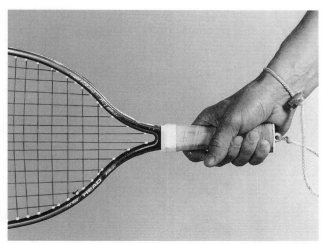

Figure 1.2. Correct grip size

oversized racquet frames (which are normally more expensive) have been judged as a must for the competitive player, but are not essential for the beginning player. A good quality racquet can be purchased for as little as $30. Racquet prices, depending on the materials used, can range as high as $300, and are obviously marketed for the serious competitor.

■ The Uniform

Unless an instructor or tournament director demands a specific uniform, there are no rules regarding the color or design of clothing for playing the game. Generally, clothing should be comfortable allowing one to move easily. Any properly fitting court shoe that does not have a sole composition that will mark the floor is recommended. Racquetball is a game that requires quickness in stopping and starting movements, therefore it is important to acquire proper support for the one's feet.

■ The Safety Equipment

The danger of incurring a serious eye injury in racquetball is genuine, due to the high velocity the racquetball travels coupled with the need for the participant to invariably glance toward the back court. Glancing toward back court is necessary in following the ball to determine the area of the court from which the return shot will be made and the nature of the opponent's shot. These quick views of the back court can't be overemphasized. Observing an opponent's shot assists a player in anticipating the direction and speed of a returned

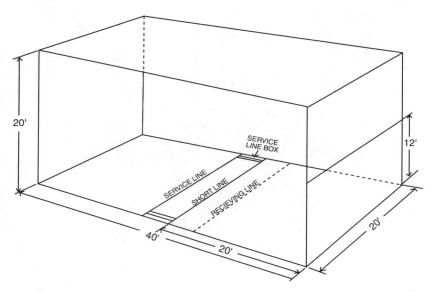

Figure 1.3. The standard four-wall racquetball court

shot, obviously improving a player's response time to the returned ball. But glancing toward the back court during play can be dangerous if one does not wear eye protection.

REMEMBER: The wearing of lensed eye glasses or guards is of paramount importance.

Although many players have participated without eye protection in court games without accident, the danger and seriousness of an eye injury in the game is well documented and considered serious enough that all players must be required to wear eye protection. **In most instructional programs and in tournament competition, the wearing of lensed eye protection is mandatory.**

Another important safety practice is to secure the wrist thong attached to the racquet around the wrist (see Figure 1.2) to avoid an accidental release of the racquet and the possibility of injuring some-one during play. In addition to the thong, some participants elect to wear a glove on their racquet hand to improve their grip for added safety and as some players believe, to contribute to racquet control and consistency of shot-making. It is a fact that the slightest shift of the racquet in one's hand can cause a shot to go awry. Sweatbands are also worn on the wrists to keep the racquet hand and glove relatively dry for a firmer grip. Headbands are employed to keep perspiration off the lensed eye protection. Another consideration of safe play includes watching the ball to know when and where to move to prevent being struck with a racquet or ball as it is returned by an opponent. **Don't crowd your opponent—avoid overswinging and opponents who overswing.**

■ The Court

The standard four-wall racquetball court (see Figure 1.3) dimensions are twenty feet wide, forty feet long, and twenty feet high with a back wall at least twelve feet high. There are six other court markings specified by the official rules. These are:

1. **Short Line**—a line parallel to the front and back walls dividing the court in half.

2. **Service Line**—a line parallel to the front and back walls located five feet in front of the short line.

3. **Service Zone**—the area between the outer edge of the short and service lines.

4. **Service Boxes**—two areas located at either end of the service zone marked with a line parallel to the side walls and eighteen inches from each side wall.

5. **Receiving Line**—a broken line parallel to and located five feet behind the short line.

6. **Drive Serve Zone**—two areas located at either end of the service zone encompassing the service boxes and marked by a line parallel to and three feet away from both side walls. (The **service boxes** are within this area.)

■ The Game

The game of racquetball is played using the same basic court and rules as paddleball and handball. To begin the game the server, while standing within the service zone lines, drops the ball to the floor within the service zone, and strikes it on the first bounce. After being struck by the server, the ball must travel in a direct line to and contact the front wall first. The rules call for the ball to rebound directly off the front wall or to either side wall prior to contacting the floor beyond (not touching) the short line. The receiver must return the ball on the first bounce to the front wall directly or indirectly (using the side walls, ceiling or back wall) without contacting the floor. Play (the rally) continues until the server or the receiver fails to return the ball legally, that is before the ball bounces twice or contacts either player. Only the individual or team (doubles) serving can score points. The individual or team that scores fifteen points first wins the game. A match consists of the best two out of three games with the tie breaking third game played to eleven.

Beginning Raquetball Study Questions

Chapter 1

1. Who is credited with founding the game of racquetball and in what year?

2. What four-wall game inspired the founder to develop racquetball?

3. Identify the four characteristics of a racquet that a player should take into consideration when purchasing a racquet.

4. Name two pieces of equipment required in racquetball to prevent what could be the most serious injuries in the game.

5. What are the dimensions of the court including the following: height, width, length, and the minimal height of the back wall?

6. Name the court marking that divides the court in half. What is the purpose of that line?

7. What is the term for the floor area between the outer edge of the line located in mid-court and the service line?

8. Identify the term assigned to the broken line parallel to and located five feet from the line that divides the court in half?

9. In what way do the basic dimensions for a racquetball court differ from those of the handball and paddleball courts?

10. To begin the game, what wall must the ball strike first and what line must it pass prior to the first bounce of the ball?

2 FUNDAMENTAL SKILLS

Compared to most racquet sports, racquetball is considered a fairly simple game that is easy to play, and the time required to play a match is usually one hour or less. To play the game reasonably well (as a beginner), one needs to learn how to strike the ball using the forehand or the backhand swings with proper mechanical form, utilizing correct speed and control. To accomplish this, the ball must always be contacted with the racquet face in the proper position. In fact, if the racquetball is hit correctly, it rebounds off the racquet with little or no spin. **The placing of spin on the ball is of little importance in this game, making the basic swings easier to master than in some racquet sports.**

■ The Grip

To assume the proper grip, the racket is held in place with the off-hand at the throat of the racquet with the thumb and forefinger, and the racquet hand is placed flat on the face of the racket. The racquet hand is then moved down the throat of the racquet grasping the handle. In this position the end of the handle should protrude about a quarter of an inch beyond the little finger (see Figure 2.1). The racket must be held so that the angle formed by the player's arm and the racquet throat is about 130 degrees. The "v" formed by the thumb and forefinger of the hand holding the racquet should be on the top of the handle (see Figure 2.2). Fingers are slightly spread on the handle to increase racquet control. To maintain control of the racquet when swinging it full force, the racquet is held only as

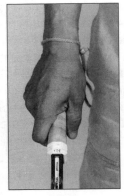

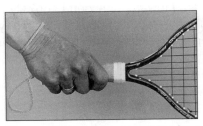

Figure 2.1. Proper grip—side view

Figure 2.2. Proper grip—top view

firmly as necessary. Applying too much pressure or "squeezing" while gripping the handle can cause undue forearm fatigue.

Slight individual differences in the striking motion will require participants to personally adjust their grip. But one very important basic mechanical fact that does not differ in the execution of the swing is that the racquet face must be kept perpendicular to the floor at the moment of contact with the ball. The racquet face must not be tilted up or down but held in a position as if it were placed flat against the front wall. The obvious exception is when one wishes to hit the ball from a low position upward or a high position downward, at which time the racquet is altered to direct the ball up or down.

■ Footwork and Body Position

A large part of the footwork and body position technique involved in racquetball is similar to the footwork and body position employed in guarding an opponent in basketball. Most of the movement in this as well as other court games is best accomplished with a sliding motion of the feet, avoiding the crossing of one foot over the other. The sliding technique is efficient and results in better body position for striking the ball. Once the proper swing of the racquet is learned, improvement in foot movement will add significantly to the participant's overall playing ability and performance.

■ Ready Position

The ready position which a player assumes to receive the serve is as much a mental state as it is a physical position. The ready position is crucial in racquetball because each error by the receiver on each return of serve attempt results in a loss of a point. Normally, the player receiving the serve assumes a position facing the front wall approximately three feet from the back wall equidistant from both side walls (see Figure 2.3). From this position one is able to move easily to cover either side of the court. Lining up at least three feet away from the back wall is necessary for another reason. A ball hit with great force will rebound off the back wall so quickly that it is to the receiver's advantage to have a three-foot lead toward mid-court to quickly assume the proper striking position to return the ball. In the ready position the receiver's feet are placed slightly wider than shoulder width apart with knees bent slightly. As a matter of fact, it is not unlike a baseball batter assuming a batting stance while waiting for the pitched ball (see Figure 2.4).

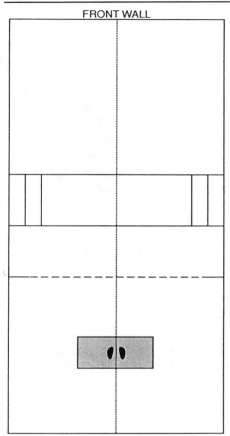

FRONT WALL

Figure 2.3. Ready position on the court—receiving the serve

Figure 2.4. Ready position

REMEMBER: While in the ready position, the racquet is held in front of the body, thumb and forefinger of the off hand placed on the throat of the racquet for support, allowing for quick movement to the forehand or backhand position while the reciever moves into position to strike the ball.

■ Pivot To Forehand and Backhand

There are several methods for assuming the forehand position from the ready position. The participant can pivot a quarter turn on either foot, resulting in the participant's facing the right side wall with the left side of the body facing the front wall. This position can also be assumed by the player executing a quick one-quarter jump-turn to face the right side wall. Assuming the backhand position requires the same movements except the participant is facing the left side wall with the right side of the body facing the front wall.

■ Moving To The Ball

Obviously, every ball hit by an opponent will not return to the area currently occupied by the participant. In this case a simple pivot or quarter jump turn will not place a player in position to attempt a shot. More often than not participants will have to move from the ready position to another area of the court to assume the forehand or backhand position necessary to execute a successful shot. Various game situations will require players to move forward, backward, right, or left before assuming a mechanically sound striking position prior to executing a shot. Although running is required at times, the recommended movement for getting into position for striking the ball consists of a quick sliding technique described earlier in the section on footwork and body position.

> **REMEMBER:** Moving to the right spot on the court and assuming the mechanically sound body position for a shot, more often than not, results in the execution of the most effective shot. Being able to anticipate the path of the ball in various shots and getting to the ball quickly to set up for the return shot on a regular basis is a difficult skill to learn.

■ The Forehand Swing

The forehand swing resembles a side-armed throwing motion. Facing the right side wall with the left side of the body facing the front wall, one bends the arm and flexes the wrist bringing the racquet head up to and near the right ear. The player's arm must be bent over ninety degrees with the elbow pointed to the back wall. Nearly all of the body weight at this point is borne on the rear foot (see Figure 2.5-a). From this initial striking position the throwing motion is simply begun by straightening the arm, rotating it, thus "driving" the racquet through the ball with a wrist snap (see Figure 2.5-d). The swing ends in a compact bent arm position (see Figure 2.5-f) to avoid hitting one's opponent with the racquet. **Don't overswing.** The proper path of the racquet is best understood if the participant imagines this movement as passing the racket parallel to the top of a flat surface about knee high. It is important to keep the head of the racquet level with the wrist to direct the ball on its intended path. During a correct swing, the body weight will shift from the back foot to the lead foot (see Figure 2.5-c). The hips

Figure 2.5. The forehand swing

The hips and shoulders will rotate from a position of facing the side wall and end at a point of facing the front wall (see Figure 2.5-e, f).

> **REMEMBER:** When done properly, the forehand swing will resemble a side armed throw, complete with follow-through. The movement terminates with the hitting arm wrapped around the front of the body and the racquet behind the left ear.

■ The Backhand Swing

The overall movement in executing the backhand swing can best be described as resembling a standard "frisbee" throw (see Figure 2.6). In preparation for this swing, face the left side wall with knees bent, feet about shoulder width apart, and toes pointing toward the left side wall. The player initiates the backhand movement by bringing the racquet across the body, ending with the head of the racquet near the left ear (see Figure 2.6-a). At full backswing the elbow of the hitting

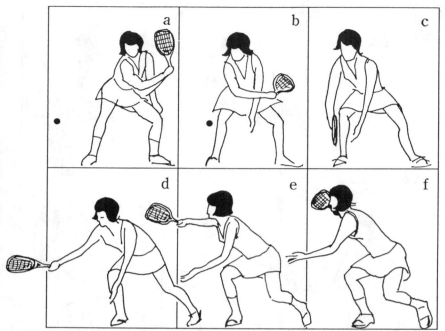

Figure 2.6. The backhand swing

arm should be pointing toward the floor. The arm is bent at the elbow in excess of 90 degrees with the wrist flexed. Most of the body weight at this moment, as in the forehand swing, is borne on the rear foot. To initiate the swing from this flexed or "cocked" position, the arm is extended sharply and rotated as in a standard "frisbee" toss. As an aid to a clearer understanding of the overall technique, one must imagine the racquet being swept parallel to the top of a flat surface (as in the forehand) while keeping the head of the racquet on the same level supported by the wrist. As in the forehand technique, the weight is shifted from the rear foot to the lead foot, rotating the hips and shoulders from facing the left side wall to facing the front wall (see Figure 2.6-f). Both the forehand and backhand swing can be practiced and improved without hitting the ball.

REMEMBER: The overall backhand swing most resembles the standard "frisbee" toss.

■ The Overhead Swing

The overhead striking motion most resembles an overhand throw (see Figure 2.7). As in the forehand, to execute the shot just straighten the arm, release the cocked wrist and contact the ball. The main differences between the overhead and the forehand motion are the upright stance which the player assumes to strike the ball and the height at which the ball is contacted. In the overhead swing the ball is contacted shoulder to head height or higher. The shots normally hit with an overhead swing are the drive or ceiling ball, each of which will be described later. Of the three basic strokes, this one is the more difficult to learn, and beginners should spend more of their practice time concentrating on the proper execution of the basic forehand and backhand swings.

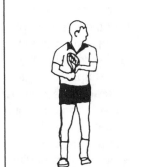

Figure 2.7. The overhead swing

The forehand, backhand, and overhand swinging motion must be practiced without the ball (swinging at an imaginary ball) until form is perfected without having to think about the individual parts of the swing. Only after this is accomplished can the necessary confidence in striking the ball with purpose be instilled in the beginning player.

■ Striking The Ball

Once the forehand and backhand swings have been sufficiently improved by practicing without the ball, begin practicing with the ball. To do this the ball is held at about arm's length and approximately twelve inches in front of the lead foot (the foot nearest the front wall). With the knees bent slightly, drop the ball and begin the swing while taking a short step forward with the lead foot. It is important that the ball be contacted in the top center of the racquet (commonly called the "sweet spot") so the ball rebounds off the racquet with appropriate force and direction. When the ball is hit correctly, a loud popping noise will result as the ball rebounds off the racquet. The object is to direct the ball in a path as near parallel to the floor as possible. If the ball is not traveling in what appears to be a parallel line to the floor after being hit, some adjustment of the grip or swing may be necessary. The ball should be contacted soon after it has begun its downward flight after the first bounce. This drill should increase one's ability to hit the ball from a low position after one bounce to a low front wall targeted area.

Chapter 2

1. Is placing a spin on the ball important in racquetball? If not, what does this mean for the beginning player learning the swing?

2. When employing the proper grip for the forehand, what is the relative distance of the little finger of the hand gripping the racquet from the end of the handle of the racquet?

3. In the proper grip of a racquet, the thumb and the forefinger of the hand holding the racquet forms a "v." Where, approximately, on the racquet handle is the "v" formed?

4. Slight individual differences for executing a successful striking motion are acknowledged. But in the swing, the position of the racquet face at the moment of contact with the ball remains the same. What is the racquet face position recommended for success?

5. What foot-movement technique is deemed most efficient, placing the body in the best position for striking the ball?

6. Why is the ready position so crucial in playing the game? Where on the court does the individual receiving the serve assume the ready position? What is the recommended racquet grip and attitude?

7. What basic footwork is recommended when assuming the forehand and backhand positions from the ready position.

8. Moving to the ball in play, other than using a simple pivot movement, is a difficult skill. A player must anticipate the path of the ball. What is the recommended movement technique to get into striking position when running is unneccesary?

9. When properly done, the forehand swing looks like a throwing motion including the follow-through. How would you describe that throwing motion? Can you recount the weight shift and footwork to properly perform the forehand swing? What is the ending or final position of the hitting arm and racquet in executing the throwing motion?

Chapter 2, *continued*

10. The overall movement of the backhand swing resembles what popular backyard recreational activity? How does the basic footwork in executing a backhand differ from that in performing the forehand? The proper technique in the backhand swing includes rotating the hips and shoulders from facing what wall to facing what other wall?

11. The overhead striking motion is described as resembling what throwing motion? Considering the two other basic strokes, forehand and backhand, how would this stroke rank in terms of learning difficulty and execution?

12. To practice striking the ball, the player drops the ball from a recommended arms length to a specific spot on the floor. How far is the arm and hand holding the ball extended and what is the recommended placement of the ball on the floor relative to the lead foot?

13. What is the recommended spot on the racquet which the ball must contact to cause it to rebound off the racquet with the intended force and direction? Where, in the height of the first bounce, should the ball be contacted to insure it is directed to a low position on the front wall so as to minimize the rebound bounce?

SERVICE AND RETURN

The serve is the method of putting the ball in play. However, its importance cannot be overstated. A well-planned and well-executed serve allows the server to remain on the offensive and maintain the best court position to win the rally and score a point. A poorly conceived and executed serve will in most cases result in a loss of serve and transfer that advantage to the opponent. The server should attempt to direct each serve into an area of the rear court where there is the least chance of an effective return, allowing the server to remain on the offensive. The type of serve and its placement should be determined through thoughtful analysis of an opponent's most glaring strengths and weaknesses in the return of serve. A significant number of points in any three-game match can accrue as a result of a series of well-planned and well-executed serves.

An opponent receiving the serve may compensate for a weakness during the course of the game by significantly moving their ready position to favor one side of the court. Therefore, keen observation of the changing ready position is essential prior to delivering each serve.

REMEMBER: Be Alert! Don't fall into the common practice of serving solely to place the ball in play.

The most successful serves in most court games are those directed toward the opponent's backhand because it is the least developed part of most players' game. As the game and match progress, it is wise to vary the direction, height, and speed of every serve. Keeping an opponent in the position of being unable to predict or anticipate the next serve should cause difficulties for most players.

The mechanics of serving the ball resemble the basic forehand striking motion. You begin in a position in the service zone facing the side wall with feet staggered but pointing toward the side wall (see Figure 3.1). When in this position the ball is dropped so that it rebounds once to the desired height for striking and directing the ball for a specific result. The direction, force, and height at which the ball is hit determines the type of serve offered. Every effort should be made to mask the intended nature of each serve to maintain the element of surprise, minimizing the opponent's ability to anticipate the intended serve.

After the serve is delivered, the server must move to a position three to four feet behind the short line in the middle of the court.While moving to this position the server glances toward the rear court to quickly determine the direction and force of the upcoming opponent's return.

Figure 3.1. Serving position

■ Basic Serves

There are four basic serves in racquetball.
1. the drive serve
2. the short lob or "garbage" serve
3. the "Z" serve
4. the deep lob serve

The greater degree of mastery of several serves and their variations can determine a participant's relative success in playing racquetball.

Drive Serve

The drive serve is generally most effective when executed from near the center of the service zone. The serve is struck on a direct line toward the front wall slightly left or right of center. The ball should rebound low off the front wall with good speed and contact the floor behind and as close to the short line as possible. It can be directed to either corner of the rear court causing a difficult return for the receiver (see Figure 3.2). The speed of this serve forces the opponent to move quickly from the ready position to the ball in either rear corner thus increasing the chance of a poor return or an error.

The effectiveness of the drive serve is determined by the amount of force (resulting in a fast moving ball) and the accuracy with which it is delivered to either corner. The force of the serve is primarily imparted by simultaneously stepping forward, accelerating the normal forehand swing, and striking the ball after a low bounce, directing it to the front wall. To develop force it is recommended that the full distance from the short line to the service line be utilized in stepping forward to develop momentum in delivering the serve. The rules allow the server to stand on the short line but not over it, and step forward on the service line but not over it when serving the ball.

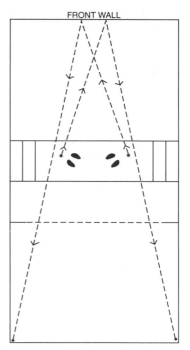

Figure 3.2. The drive serve

The accuracy of this serve is generally accomplished by controlling the racquet head position and aiming the ball to a predetermined spot, right or left of center on the front wall. Patiently waiting for the ball to start its downward flight after the bounce can contribute greatly to the accuracy of the drive serve. Consistency in locating and contacting the correct impact area on the front wall for an effective drive serve takes hours of practice. This is a difficult serve to hit with a high percentage of success.

The Deep Lob Serve

The deep lob serve's effectiveness is enhanced when it is delivered from a point near the center of the service zone or from a position in the service zone close to the side wall along which the ball is intended to travel. The serve is delivered by gently striking the ball so that it contacts the front wall at three-fourths of the height of the front wall, causing it to rebound in a slow arc to the deep rear court (see Figure 3.3). When the ball is served from near mid-court, it should be angled off the front wall in a way that it is directed to either of the rear corners. When the ball is served from a position within the service zone close to either side wall, it should travel as near the side wall as possible to

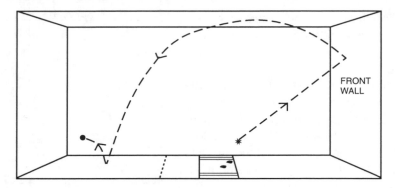

Figure 3.3. The deep lob serve

the rear corner on the side of the court from which it was delivered. To increase the effectiveness of this serve, one should direct the ball in such a way that it glances off the side wall just before it bounces and contacts the back wall. This causes the ball to loose momentum and reduces the height of the bounce, making an effective return most difficult.

To properly execute this serve, which requires extreme control, the racquet movement and momentum should originate from the rotation of the hips and shoulders rather than from the arm and flexed wrist. This technique provides better racquet control. In delivering the serve, the ball should be released from approximately chest height and contacted at the apex of the bounce (in the hip to chest level). This enables the server to guide the racquet under the ball and with a partial swing propel it toward the intended target high on the front wall.

The Short Lob ("Garbage") Serve

The short lob or "garbage" serve is similar to the deep lob serve in pace and execution. The serve is correctly performed by striking the ball so that it contacts the front wall approximately two-thirds of the height of the front wall, rebounding in a slow arc and contacting the floor between the short line and the broken safety line (see Figure 3.4). It should then bounce in a high arc and lose most of its momentum just prior to contacting the back wall. This serve forces the receiver to attempt a return of the ball from a chest high position, reducing the chance of an effective offensive return.

The body mechanics for delivering the garbage serve are similar to the deep lob serve. As in the deep lob serve, the force for the half-swing should emanate from the hips and shoulders and the ball should be struck at chest level. It is helpful on all serves to target a spot on the front wall and attempt to direct the ball to that spot.

REMEMBER: The swing for the deep lob and the short lob ("garbage") is considerably slower than the normal swing. It consists of a controlled half-swing getting the majority of its momentum from the rotation of the hips and shoulders—not the arm and flexed wrist.

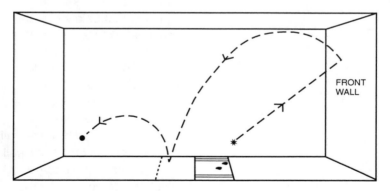

Figure 3.4. The short lob

The "Z" Serve

Another difficult but effective serve when delivered correctly is the "Z" serve. This serve will have a higher degree of success if executed from near the center of the court. The "Z" serve is directed so the ball contacts the front wall near either corner, rebounds off the side wall nearest that corner, travels on a sharp angle across the court and strikes the floor in the opposite rear corner. The ball bounds into and ricochets off the opposite side wall completing a "Z" pattern formed by its total flight after initially contacting the front wall.

When hitting the "Z" serve it is important to remember the angles involved to make the serve effective. When the right handed player attempts to hit the "Z" serve to the right front corner, the ball should be dropped closer than normal to the player's body in order to establish the proper initial angle for sending the shot on its "Z" route. The swing for this serve is the normal forehand drive swing, and the force with which it is delivered can be varied to keep the opponent off balance. Care must be taken to contact the front wall before the ball rebounds to the side wall, otherwise a sideout occurs. This is a common error when performing this serve. The position (height) which the ball needs to contact the front wall will depend on the pace with which the serve is delivered. The greater the force with which the serve is hit, the lower one should target the ball on the front wall.

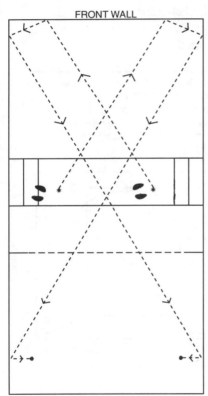

FRONT WALL

Figure 3.5. The "Z" serve

■ Serving Tactics

As the server, you have greater control of the situation than at any other time in the rally.

REMEMBER: Use the serve wisely. There are a variety of actions a server must consider as a part of an overall plan to increase the effectiveness of the server and keep control of the rally

1. Develop a serve or combination of serves that can be executed with confidence. Use these as often as possible, keeping the opponent's return of the serve deficiencies in mind.

2. Before serving, knowledge of the opponent's readiness to receive particular serves can be determined with a glance to the back court. Observation of an opponent's court position helps to determine if a specific serve would be more effective at this particular time in the match.

3. Serving the ball to solely put it in play reduces the over-all effectiveness of being the server. Plan to deliver each serve to an area of the court based on the return of serve abilities of the opponent as well as the current game and match situation. This involves an evolving game plan using basic serves and variations of these serves.

4. Opponents can be kept off balance by serving in an unpredictable pattern to either corner of the rear court in a series of serves. The objective is to keep an opponent in back court and on the defensive so the server can maintain the offensive mid- to front-court position after each serve.

5. The general nature and speed of serves should be con-tinually altered. This makes it difficult for an opponent to assume a set position and make an effective return.

6. Don't hurry the serve. Having complete control of delivering the ball to win a point while serving is a distinct advantage.

7. After the serve is delivered the server must move to a position three to four feet behind the short line in the middle of the court. At that point the server glances toward the rear court to determine, as soon as possible, the direction and force of the opponent's return.

8. If the first serve is a fault, the second serve should be one which can be executed with a high degree of success. Don't loose the serve on a double fault!

9. It is good strategy for the server to attempt a scoring shot off the return of serve if the opponent's shot is weak.

10. It is wise to initiate the serve from the same basic position in the service zone as often as possible. This helps conceal one's intended serve.

11. To avoid a fault in doubles, the server's partner must be in the service box before the serve is initiated.

■ Receiving the Serve

When receiving the serve, assume the ready position—facing the front wall with the feet comfortably apart and parallel to the front wall. Using the proper grip, hold the racquet at waist height with the opposite hand lightly supporting the throat of the racquet (see section on ready position and Figure 2.4). The best court position for receiving the serve is approximately three feet from the back wall equidistant from either side wall (see Figure 2.3). Feet should be flat on the floor (as opposed to being on the balls of the feet) with the knees bent and body weight forward. This position allows for instantaneous movement to any area of the court the server directs the ball. After reaching the area where the ball is served, quickly assume a proper striking position for the return. If the server delivers a weak offering and the receiver is in position, an offensive shot should be attempted. If the serve is troublesome for the receiver, a defensive shot should be executed to allow the receiver to gain the center court position. This is best accomplished with a well-placed passing or ceiling shot.

When preparing to receive the serve and in the ready position, the receiver should concentrate on the overall movement of the server in delivering each serve. After carefully observing the server for a number of serves, the receiver may chance upon a clue in that movement which foretells the nature of an upcoming serve. With such information, the important natural advantage of the server could be somewhat reduced.

REMEMBER: In most cases, the best return of service is the ceiling shot (see figure 6.6).

Chapter 3

1. What are the principal advantages the server enjoys? How does the server determine what type of serve is best used in playing each new opponent?

2. How would you describe the mechanics of executing the serve? What is gained by the server masking each serve?

3. The server, after delivering the serve, should immediately move from the serving zone to a recommended area of the court. Identify the area of the court to which the server is to move. What is the stated purpose for the server's movement to the recommended area?

4. Name the four basic serves in raquetball.

5. What is the distinguishing feature of the drive serve? What basic movement technique is recommended to impart the necessary force in delivering an effective drive serve? Identify the recommended area of the serving zone from which a server is most likely to deliver an effective drive serve.

6. The deep lob and the short lob (or half-lob or garbage serve) serves are similar in terms of pace and execution. What is the distinguishing feature (end result) of these two serves? Can you describe the body movement technique the server uses to develop racquet movement and momentum in delivering the lob serves?

7. How does the height of the ball at the moment of racquet contact with the ball in the lob serve differ from the drive serve?

Chapter 3, *continued*

8. What makes the "Z" serve one of the more difficult but effective serves, if delivered correctly? Diagram the path of the ball on a well executed "Z" serve.

9. The height with which the ball contacts the front wall on the "Z" serve is dictated by the force with which the ball is delivered. How does the force applied to the ball differ when the ball is contacted at a lower level as compared to one struck at a higher level of the front wall?

10. When serving the ball, what is recommended relative to:

a. Your knowledge of an opponents capabilities?

b. The opponents location in rear court for receiving the serve?

c. The position to be taken by the server after delivering the serve?

d. The general nature and speed of each serve?

e. The recommended position in the serving zone for initiating the serve?

f. The first serve resulting in a fault?

11. What constitutes the ready position in preparation for receiving the serve? Identify the recommended position on the rear court where the receiver is to assume the ready position.

12. Identify the best return of service and state the rationale for executing it.

4 DOUBLES PLAY

In doubles, the players on each team should determine which side of the court each team member will cover. Once a positioning scheme is established, the players assume this formation during their serve, while receiving the serve, and during play. Two commonly used styles of doubles court coverage schemes are the **side-by-side** and the **front and back** methods.

In the **side-by-side** method of play, each team member is responsible for approximately one-half of the court divided front to back down the center (see Figure 4.1). There are times when it is necessary for one player on the team to momentarily cover part of the partner's assigned court area. At the moment the ball is served, the partner not receiving the serve must move forward to a position behind and near the service line, slightly toward the center of the court. From this position one is able to cover the total front court until the partner, who is returning the serve, can assume his/her originally assigned half of the front court. When the ball is returned down the center of the court, it is best played by the player on the left half of the court (if right handed) who can play the ball with a forehand swing. If the team is made up of a left-handed player on the left and a right-handed player on the right, the player in the best position to play the ball or with the strongest backhand should play the ball down the center of the court.

As a general rule in side-by-side play, the better skilled of the two players assumes responsibility for the left side of the court. But, if one

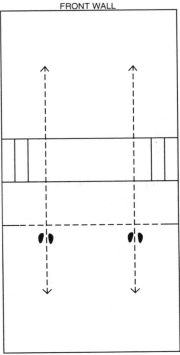

Figure 4.1. Doubles court coverage side-by-side

of the players is left handed, that individual normally plays the left side so that both players can return difficult corner shots with the forehand.

In the **front and back** method of play, each player is assigned to a diagonal area on either side of a dissecting line running from the front left corner to the rear right corner (see Figure 4.2). The right-side player is responsible for the front court area shots and low-angle shots in the left-front corner area. The left-side player covers the rear court shots, passing shots, back wall shots, and high angling shots off either wall. As in side-by-side method of play, both receivers initially assume the ready position three feet from the back wall and at least five to seven feet from either side wall. From this position, any serve to either side of the court will be played by the player occupying that side. Once the ball is served, the player receiving the serve moves toward the area of the court to which the ball has been directed and assumes the correct striking position for a return shot. As indicated earlier in the discussion of the side-by-side scheme, **the partner of the teammate receiving the serve moves forward to the center area of the court to cover the open center/front court until the receiver is able to assume the basic assigned position for the front and back scheme of doubles play.**

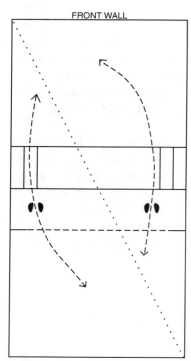

Figure 4.2. Doubles court coverage—front and back

REMEMBER: In doubles, with four players on the court, play is fast and the court is crowded. This can be dangerous and calls for careful movement and compact swings to avoid injury.

Chapter 4

1. A number of schemes for responsibility in covering the court in doubles play can be concocted. Name the two commonly used doubles play court coverage methods.

2. Diagram the two styles of covering the court in doubles play discussed in this chapter.

3. What is the importance and purpose of doubles players selecting and practicing a court responsibility plan?

4. In the side-by-side method of play there are times when it is necessary for one player of the doubles team to momentarily cover a part of their partners assigned court. What is the recommended action of the partner not receiving the serve, once the serve is directed to their partner?

5. In the side-to-side method of play, if both partners are right-handed players, what is the preferred side of the court for the better player of the doubles team? What characteristic, beyond skill of the partners, could determine the line-up of partners in the side-by-side formation?

6. In what area of the court do partners receiving the serve assume the ready position when playing the front and back scheme in doubles play?

7. Briefly, outline the responsibilities for the right and left side players in the front and back method of doubles play.

8. How do the actions of the doubles partner of the teammate receiving the serve differ in the front and back method from the side-by-side method of dividing court responsibility?

9. Doubles play can be hurried and cause court congestion creating dangerous situations. What should be done to minimize injuries during hurried and crowded play?

5 BACK-WALL AND CORNER PLAY

Two of the more advanced fundamental skills in the game involve participants moving to play the ball off the back wall and out of the back corners. The same forehand, backhand, and overhead swings apply in the back wall and corner shot situations. Therefore, the prime objective in playing the ball in these situations is efficiency of movement to the location on the floor where the shot will be executed. This requires a knowledge of the bouncing properties of the ball and the geometry of the path of the ball as the ball rebounds and bounces off the front, side, and back walls, as well as the ceiling and floor surfaces. Once the beginning player learns the basic forehand and backhand techniques it is time to begin working on back-wall and corner play.

■ Back-Wall Play

One of the more important fundamental and difficult aspects of the game for beginners is playing the ball after it bounds off the back wall. As difficult as the skills of back-wall play are to acquire, they must be learned if a player is to advance beyond the beginning level. Many beginners avoid learning back-wall play and simply drive the ball against the back wall after it has rebounded off the back wall which is a weak and ineffective shot and should be used sparingly as a rally saving play.

A back-wall shot consists of returning a ball that has rebounded off the back wall before the ball touches the floor twice. During the course of any one game a player is faced with a number of hard-hit shots that are best played off the back wall allowing the ball to rebound to reduce its speed. Once the ball has rebounded off the back wall and is traveling toward the front wall, any of the basic shots can be used to take advantage of the situation. A ball which is traveling toward the front wall (after rebounding off the back wall) is easier to hit and control than a ball which approaches the receiver at high speed directly off the front wall. In most cases the player must strike the ball on the fly after the ball has rebounded off the back wall. The most difficult part of back-wall play is the timely movement of the body and feet into proper position to strike the ball. As explained earlier, a common judgment error for beginning players is taking a position too close to the back wall, allowing the ball to rebound off the back wall out of reach for the return.

Another common fault in back-wall play execution is attempting to strike the ball too soon, that is before it has time to rebound to a knee- or ankle-high position. The player must be patient after moving to the ball and assuming the striking position, waiting for the ball to drop to a knee-high level or lower.

The speed, height, and angle with which the ball contacts the back wall determines the ultimate location of the basic striking position for the shot. The player must carefully follow the flight of the ball toward the back wall and at the same time determine the eventual position for striking the rebounding ball while moving quickly with it. As the ball rebounds off the back wall, pivot and slide the feet moving parallel with the ball toward the front wall and at the same time prepare to strike the ball as it descends toward the floor (see Figure 5.1). For the most effective shot, assume the basic striking position with the knees bent. The fine judgment necessary in successful back-wall play in

Figure 5.1. Back wall play sequence

most cases is often slow in developing and requires game playing experience and hours of practice.

REMEMBER: During practice and playing sesions give throughtful study and observation of the geometry of a four-wall court and rebounding quaities of the ball. In time, the ability to determine the best court position to strike the ball will become automatic.

■ Corner Play

Another difficult movement skill for most players to learn is playing the ball after it has bounded into either of the back corners of the court. When this occurs the ball rebounds in a predictable fashion given a similar set of circumstances (speed and angle of flight). Usually, when the ball contacts one of the side walls before rebounding off the back wall, the ball bounds toward the center of the court. When this situation develops, simply face the corner and remain in place, waiting for the ball, observing it as it rebounds off the side and back walls prior to sliding into

Figure 5.2. Corner play sequence

position to attempt the shot (see Figure 5.2). With sufficient game-playing experience and a good sense of the geometry of the situation, some players are able to turn their backs to the ball and go to the prime spot to make the shot. **For beginners we recommend keeping the ball in view at all times.** In situations where the ball contacts the back wall before rebounding to the side wall, the ball will usually rebound along the same path it was traveling prior to contacting the back wall (it will, in most cases, be moving parallel to the side wall). This requires the player to assume a position closer to the side wall to be in the correct place to make an effective return. However, it is not necessary to get nearer to the side wall than one-arm-plus-racquet length in order to reach the ball.

Chapter 5

1. Playing the ball bounding off the back wall and the rear corners of the court requires advanced skills and knowledge. What skills and knowledge must be developed to become relatively successful in playing the ball in these situations?

2. What fundamental skills should beginning racquetball players develop prior to working on back wall and rear corner play?

3. Judging the speed and angle of a hard hit ball that will rebound off the back wall can be difficult. After making that judgement, what is the most difficult task that faces the player responsible for returning the ball?

4. Two common faults occur in back-wall play, one has to do with court position and the other has to do with striking the ball. Briefly, what are these two faults?

5. What three flight characteristics of the ball determine the ultimate floor position at which the striking position is established to play the ball off the back wall?

6. Playing the ball in and around the corners of the rear court can be as difficult and may be more difficult than simple back-wall play. In playing the ball in the rear corners, what should beginning players do with regards to visual contact with the ball? How does the footwork in executing the corner ball play differ from playing the ball straight off the back wall?

6 BASIC SHOTS AND SHOT SELECTION

Of the many shots in racquetball, there are four considered basic to playing a varied and technically sound game. From these shots, any number of variations can be developed. The basic shots are:

1. the kill
2. the pass
3. the ceiling
4. the drop

All of these basic shots can be made with either the forehand, backhand, or overhead swing.

■ Kill Shot

A consistent and effective kill shot is one of the more difficult shots to master in racquetball. The objective of the kill shot is to strike the ball low on the front wall so that it is practically unplayable by an opponent. Most kill shots are best executed when the ball is permitted to drop to the lowest possible level (six to twelve inches from the floor) prior to contacting the ball. Attempted kill shots on balls positioned above the level of the knee are less likely to be successful.

The technique for executing the kill shot begins with the player assuming the basic striking position, facing the side wall with toes pointing toward the side wall. The arm is bent and the wrist is flexed so that the racquet head is behind the ear. The striking motion—a full-arm swing—is made with the body bent forward at the waist with the knees bent. Contact with the ball is made in line with the lead foot. Because of the precision necessary to execute this shot, a great deal of practice is required before any consistency is acquired.

The kill shot can be hit directly to the front wall, or angled off either side wall to the front wall, or angled off the front wall to either side wall. Kill shots can be initiated while the ball is in flight (volley), immediately after the ball strikes the floor (the half-volley), or after a full bounce. They can be executed as the ball is coming off the ceiling, off either side wall, or off the back wall.

The various kill shots are hit in essentially the same way, but the specific kill shot to be used in different game situations is dictated by an opponent's court position and the score of the game. Considering the difficulty of mastering the kill shot, it can be unproductive for most players to attempt too many kill shots. Also, it is not advisable to attempt to kill from a poor technical striking position or court position, or when an opponent has center-court position. As a matter of technique, it is important to avoid striking down on a high bounding ball when attempting to execute the kill shot. Doing so reduces the effectiveness of the shot, since a downward striking path causes the ball to rebound higher than usual, providing a relatively easy return.

REMEMBER: The correct and most effective method of executing the shot is to allow the ball to drop as low as possible and direct the ball toward a low spot on the front wall on as near a parallel line to the floor as possible.

Direct Front-Wall Kill

In the direct front-wall kill, the ball travels from the point of impact off the racquet directly to the front wall without contacting either side wall (see Figure 6.1). This shot is effective when it travels parallel and near either side wall or diagonally across the court. This particular kill shot, although difficult, requires the least amount of skill to execute relative to other kill shots, and therefore should be utilized by the beginner to the fullest. However, to successfully execute the shot, one must assume a good basic striking position and allow the ball to drop as low as possible before it is contacted.

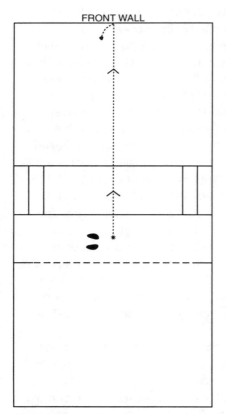

FRONT WALL

Figure 6.1. Direct front-wall kill

Side-Wall/Front-Wall Kill (Pinch Shot)

The side-wall/front-wall kill shot, also known as the pinch shot, is directed to either side wall after which the ball rebounds to the front wall (see Figure 6.2). This specific kill shot is altered by contacting the side wall from a few inches to several feet from the corner (wide pinch) which changes the angle the ball travels to the front wall. The relative position of the shot maker and the opponent will dictate the amount of angle to be used. If an opponent appears to be anticipating a certain angle shot by occupying a specific court position, simply alter the angle of the flight of the ball toward the side wall placing the ball as far away from the opponent as possible.

The mechanics of executing the side-wall/front-wall kill

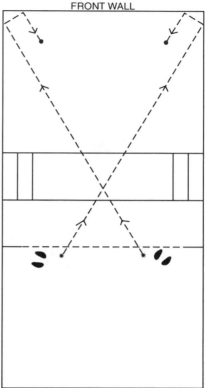

Figure 6.2. Side-wall/front-wall kill (pinch shot)

involve pivoting slightly and stepping with the lead foot toward a targeted spot on the side wall to which the ball is to be hit. In executing this shot the ball can be contacted further back than the normal striking position. Again, as in all kill shots, it is recommended that the ball be contacted when it is in a low position, as near the floor as possible.

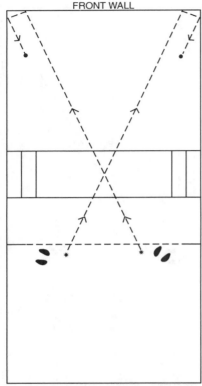

FRONT WALL

Figure 6.3. Front-wall/side-wall kill

Front-Wall/Side-Wall Kill

In the front-wall/side-wall kill, the ball is directed at an angle so the ball glances off the front wall toward either side wall (see Figure 6.3). Once the ball is hit, it contacts the front wall a few inches to a few feet from the corner to which it was directed and upon impact angles to the targeted opposite side wall. As mentioned earlier, to make kill shots the basic forehand or backhand striking position is assumed, followed by a full swing while advancing the lead foot toward the targeted spot on the front wall.

Cut-off Kill (Volley)

The cut-off kill, or volley, is a shot in which the player sacrifices good court position by quickly moving toward the front wall and strikes or blocks the ball on its rebound off the front wall, near the front wall, before the first bounce (see Figure 6.4). This shot is most effective when an opponent appears unprepared and off balance in the back court

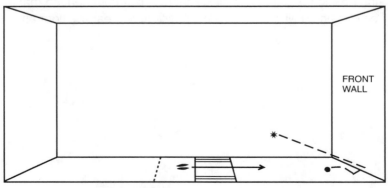

FRONT WALL

Figure 6.4. The cut-off kill (volley)

following a weak return (such as making a saving shot by hitting the ball against the back wall in order to return it to the front wall). This shot does not have to be directed to the front wall as low or with as much force as other kill shots due to the surprise element involved. The cut-off kill is most likely to be successful if the ball is contacted in flight between the level of one's waist and ankle. Of course, the lower in flight the ball is contacted the better chance of the volley being a successful shot.

■ Passing Shot

The passing shot is one of the most frequently used shots in racquetball, particularly in the singles game. It is an effective offensive shot because it does not have to be executed with great precision to achieve a good result. The passing shot must be hit on a low trajectory with sufficient speed to travel by the opponent on the right or left side, hopefully bouncing at least twice before contacting the back wall (see Figure 6.5). In most cases, the lower the trajectory and the greater the force with which a pass shot is hit, the greater it's effectiveness. The speed and low placement of the ball hit directly along either side wall or angled to hit the side wall out of reach of the opponent will prove difficult to return. The appropriate time to use the passing shot is when an opponent is in the mid-court or near either side wall. If an opponent is situated deeper than mid-court the shot tends to lose its effectiveness. A passing shot is normally executed from the basic forehand or backhand striking position, but with practice can be delivered by an overhead stroke if the situation presents itself.

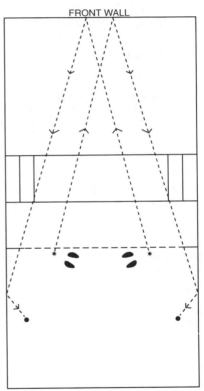

Figure 6.5. The passing shot

■ The Ceiling Shot

In racquetball the ceiling shot is basically a defensive shot. Coupled with the ability to play the ball off the back wall, effective use of the ceiling shot is what distinguishes advanced and intermediate players from beginning racquetball players. The ceiling shot is accomplished by directing the ball with an upward motion of the racquet, causing the ball to contact the ceiling approximately one foot from the top of the front wall (see Figure 6.6). The ball moves from that point on the ceiling to the front wall and rebounds at a sharp angle toward the floor bounding in a high arc toward the back wall, ending with the ball contacting the floor near but not touching the back wall. A well-executed ceiling shot is designed to move an opponent to the back court to play the ball and hopefully stifle the opponent's ability to make an offensive return.

REMEMBER: In general, the best return of a successfully executed ceiling shot is another ceiling shot.

To execute the ceiling shot the racquet face must be tilted at a 45 degree angle to the ceiling. The racquet movement must be a smooth upward motion. Rotating the hips and shoulders provides added force to the racquet, assisting in correct placement and pace of the shot. These characteristics of the shot are more important than sheer power for successful execution. Strive to hit the ball with enough force to cause the ball to carry to the back wall on its second bounce. It is important to contact the ball on line with the lead shoulder (one nearest the front wall) on either the forehand or backhand. The basic path of the swing follows a line from the floor to the juncture of the front wall and the ceiling and at an angle of about 45 degrees.

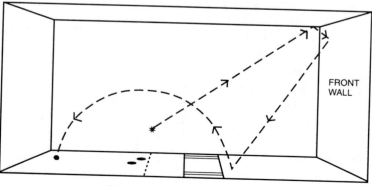

Figure 6.6. The ceiling ball

■ The Drop Shot

The drop shot is best described as a soft change-of-pace shot, usually directed to the left or right front corner (see Figure 6.7). With the lively nature of the ball, this shot requires finesse which is gained through a great deal of practice before it can be used in a game plan with any degree of success.

This shot is most effective when one's opponent is occupying the rear third of the court, and it is initiated from the center- or a front-court position. The objective of this shot is to cause your opponent to travel a great distance quickly to reach the ball for a return. If by chance the opponent returns the drop shot, he/she will be in poor front court position and out of position for the next shot. The forehand or back-hand swinging motion required for a drop shot consists of a slow, compact arm movement using little or no wrist action. A continuation of the swing on the follow-through on this shot is important to impart the desired force and direction the ball is to travel. As in most racquet-ball shots, the nearer the ball to be returned is to the floor, the greater the chance it will be a winning shot.

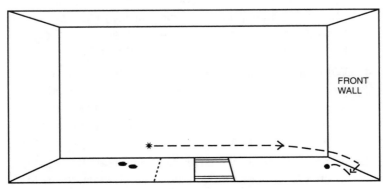

Figure 6.7. The drop shot

■ Shot Selection

In order to enjoy relative success in playing beginning racquetball, it is important to understand the technique and to be able to execute all of the basic shots. Just as important is knowing when and where to use these shots in game situations.

REMEMBER: A good general rule for shot placement is, at the time of the shot, to direct the ball as far away from your opponent's court position as possible.

The following shot recommendations for stated game situations should become an integral part of one's racquetball game:

1. The **ceiling shot** is the best return of serve and should be used 50 to 70 percent of the time.

2. **Kill shot** attempts are most successful when executed from the mid-court position.

3. It is preferable to direct the ball to the front wall first when attempting an offensive shot from the back court, especially when your opponent is in the front court. This forces an opponent to react quickly to the re-bounding ball and, in most cases, will remove him or her from the all important center court position.

4. When you are occupying a position in front court and the opponent is located in the back court, it is good strategy to direct a low shot toward one of the front corners, keeping the ball in the front court (a **drop, cut-off kill, or pinch** shot).

5. In most cases, an offensive shot should be attempted when a full swing can be taken at a ball which drops to knee height or lower.

6. **Passing shots** are most effective when an opponent is near either side wall or in the mid-court position.

Chapter 6

1. What are the four basic fundamental racquetball shots for a technically sound game?

2. What is the objective of the kill shot? What is the recommended height the ball should be contacted to ensure a successful kill shot?

3. In the technique of executing the kill shot, where, relative to the lead foot, should the ball be contacted? The specific kill shot used in different game situations is dictated by two factors. What are these?

4. Which of the four variations of the kill shot is the least difficult and is recommended as the one to be used by beginning player?

5. One of the variations of the kill shot is uniquely entitled "pinch shot." Diagram the path the ball travels in this shot from the time it is contacted to the first bounce of the ball.

6. In a surprise move to catch an opponent off-guard, one uses the cut-off kill, in which the ball is contacted in the air (a volley) before it bounces. At what relative level is the ball contacted for optimum success?

7. With that force and at what level is the ball struck to increase the effectiveness of the passing shot? What is the appropriate situation to use the passing shot as it relates to the location of an opponent in a singles match?

8. What is the purpose of the ceiling shot? At what point on the ceiling of the court is the ball directed when executing a successful ceiling shot? What is the best return of a successfully executed ceiling shot?

Chapter 6, *continued*

9. In executing the ceiling shot, what is the recommended angle of the face of the racquet in relation to the ceiling? Should the ceiling shot be hit by contacting the ball on line with the lead shoulder, the one nearest to the front wall in the forehand, or the backhand or both?

10. Describe the unique stroke characteristics in executing the ceiling shot and the reason this motion is more important than sheer power.

11. a. What is the best return of serve which should be used fifty to seventy percent of the time?

     b. Where on the court are the most successful kill shots initiated?

     c. When you occupy the front court and your opponent is in the rear court, good shot strategy dictates what shots? Why?

     d. When, relative to your opponents court position, is the best time to employ the passing shot?

12. What is the basic overall goal (strategy) for the placement of each shot, as it relates to your opponents position on the court?

7 PRACTICE DRILLS, SELF-TESTING, AND EVALUATION

In order to evaluate the acquisition of fundamental skills, the following simple skill tests are offered. There are no standardized tests for racquetball skills, but the battery presented below will provide good basic feedback on progress made at any given time. The tests can also serve as practice drills for developing the basic skills needed to play racquetball. The individual tests include the fundamental skills of serving, back-wall and ceiling play from both the forehand and backhand sides. As you practice and play, it is a good idea to test and record your progress on a weekly basis. All attempts in the tests or drills that contact the lines marking the targeted area are recorded as being successful.

Drive and Short Lob ("Garbage") Serve

1. Using masking tape or other material 1" to 2" in width that temporarily marks the floor, outline a three foot square in each of the rear corners of the court.

2. Assume the appropriate position in the service zone for the drive or garbage serve.

3. Execute either a drive or garbage serve and attempt to land the ball **on the second bounce** in one of the outlined target areas.

4. Note the number of successful attempts after ten trials.

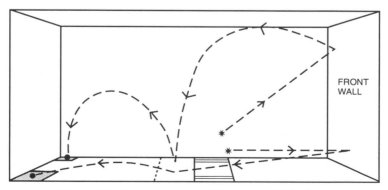

Figure 7.1. Drive and short lob serve drill/test

Be sure to attempt both serves an equal number of times to each corner targeted area.

5. A good score for a beginner in attempting each of these serves would be a total of five successful attempts out of ten trials.

Deep Lob Serve

1. Using masking tape or other material 1" to 2" in width that temporarily marks the floor, outline a five-foot square area on the side wall in each rear corner (see Figure 7.2).

2. Assume the appropriate position in the service zone for the lob serve.

3. Execute the lob serve so that it contacts the front wall three-fourths of the way up, rebounding in a slow arc to the left or right rear corner.

4. Note the number of times the ball hits the targeted five-foot square area on the side wall **before contacting the floor.**

5. A good score for a beginner would be three successful attempts out of ten trials.

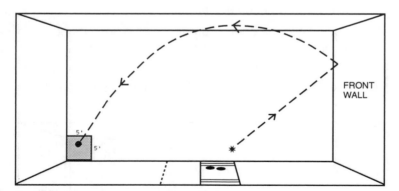

Figure 7.2. The deep lob serve drill/test

Off-the-Back-Wall Kill

1. Using masking tape or other material 1" to 2" in width that temporarily marks the front wall, mark a line along the width of the front wall one and one-half feet up from the floor (see Figure 7.3).

2. Stand five feet from the back wall in the center of the court and toss the ball about waist high against the back wall.

3. As the ball strikes the back wall, pivot into a forehand (or backhand) striking position and slide toward the front wall with the ball as it rebounds off the back wall and contacts the floor.

4. Slide the feet and adjust the body position while waiting for the ball to drop to knee height or lower near the lead leg, which is the prime striking position.

5. Strike the ball and direct it so that it contacts the front wall between the floor and the marked area.

6. A good score for a beginner would be five successful attempts out of ten trials.

Once you are able to consistently hit directly to the targeted area on the front wall, attempt to improve your accuracy by hitting either side wall before the ball contacts the marked area on the front wall.

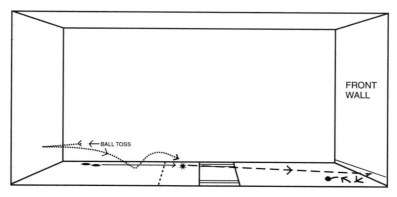

Figure 7.3. Kill off the back wall drill/test

Ceiling Ball Rally

1. Stand in the rear court and direct the ball to the ceiling (see Figure 7.4).

2. As the ball rebounds toward the back court, adjust court position to strike the ball, attempting to repeat the ceiling ball return.

3. Continue executing ceiling ball returns until the ball either bounces twice or the return does not contact the ceiling.

4. During the return, the ball can hit either the ceiling or the front wall first (although ceiling first is preferred) as long as the ball contacts both the ceiling and the front wall.

5. The score is determined by the number of successful returns made before the ball either bounces twice or fails to contact the ceiling or the front wall on the return.

6. A good score for a beginner is ten successive returns in a row in any one of five repetitions of the test.

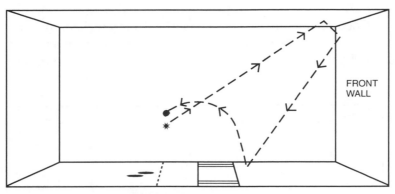

Figure 7.4. Ceiling ball rally drill/test

■ Advanced Drills

As one's skills progress, an effort should be made to practice drills that resemble game situations. The following two drills provide excellent practice for the more highly skilled beginners.

Forehand and Backhand Drive/Kill Off the Back Wall

1. Position yourself five feet from the back wall close to either rear corner (see Figure 7.5).
2. Toss the ball at medium speed toward the floor in a downward direction, striking the floor approximately one foot from the back wall. After the ball contacts the floor it rebounds into the back wall, ricocheting toward the front wall.
3. As the ball drops in flight to the prime striking height, the player slides forward and assumes the proper striking position. The player strikes the ball before it contacts the floor for the second time because it has already bounced off the floor once.

This drill can be used to perform the drive, direct front-wall kill, or the pinch shot. It is an excellent drill to learn and develop the sliding motion required to get to the proper court position and to assume the optimum body position for striking the ball.

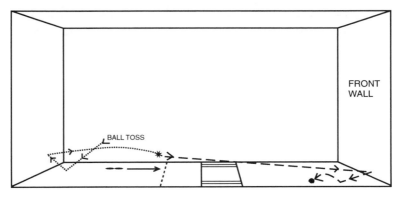

Figure 7.5. Advanced drive or kill off the back wall drill

■ Short or Mid-Length Ceiling Ball Return

1. Assume a position in the backcourt. Hit a ceiling ball that carries short of the back wall (see Figure 7.6).

2. After the ball bounces and drops toward the floor in the backcourt, attempt to make an offensive shot (a kill, pass, or drop) by waiting for the ball to drop to knee or ankle level before striking it on the fly.

There is a large degree of difficulty in this shot due to the angle and speed of the descending ball. The drill is helpful in that this set of circumstances occurs often in play, and practice is needed to develop proper footwork and timing to execute an offensive shot off a fly ball.

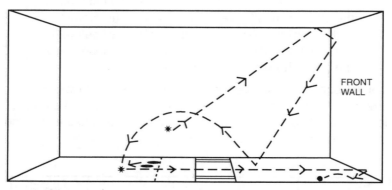

FRONT WALL

Figure 7.6. Advanced short- or mid-length ceiling ball return drill

8 RULES AND LANGUAGE OF THE GAME

1 - The Game

Rule 1.1 Types of Games

Racquetball may be played by two or four players. When played by two it is called singles and when played by four, doubles. A non-tournament variation of the game that is played by three players is called cutthroat.

Rule 1.2 Description

Racquetball is a competitive game in which a strung racquet is used to serve and return the ball.

Rule 1.3 Objective

The objective is to win each rally by serving or returning the ball so the opponent is unable to keep the ball in play. A rally is over when a player (or team in doubles) is unable to hit the ball before it touches the floor twice, is unable to return the ball in such a manner that it touches the front wall before it touches the floor, or when a hinder is called.

Rule 1.4 Points and Outs

Points are scored only by the serving side when it serves an irretrievable serve (an ace) or wins a rally. Losing the serve is called a sideout in singles. In doubles, when the first server loses the serve it is called a hand-out and when the second server loses the serve it is a sideout.

Rule 1.5 Match, Game and Tiebreaker

A match is won by the first side winning two games. The first two games of a match are played to 15 points. If each side wins one game, a tiebreaker game is played to 11 points.

Rule 1.6 Doubles Team

(a) A doubles team shall consist of two players who meet either the age requirements or player classification requirements to participate in a particular division of play. A team with different skill levels must play the division of the player with the higher level of ability. When playing in an adult age division, the team must play in the division of the younger player. When playing in a junior age division, the team must play in the division of the older player.

(b) A change in playing partners may be made so long as the first match of the posted team has not begun. For this purpose only the match will be considered started once the teams have been called to the court. The team must notify the tournament director of the change prior to the beginning of the match.

Rule 1.7 Consolation Matches

(a) Each entrant shall be entitled to participate in a minimum of two matches. Therefore, losers of their first match shall have the opportunity to compete in a consolation bracket of their own division. In draws less than seven players, a round robin may be offered. See Rule 5.5 about how to determine the winner of a round robin event.

(b) Consolation matches may be waived at the discretion of the tournament director, but this waiver must be in writing on the tournament application.

(c) Preliminary consolation matches will be two of three games to 11 points. Semifinal and final matches will follow the regular scoring format.

2 - Courts and Equipment

Rule 2.1 Court Specifications

The specifications for the standard four-wall racquetball court are:

(a) Dimensions. The dimensions shall be 20 feet wide, 40 feet long and 20 feet high, with a back wall at least 12 feet high. All surfaces shall be in play, with the exception of any gallery opening or surfaces designated as court hinders.

(b) Markings. Racquetball courts shall be marked with lines 1 1/2 inch wide as follows:

1. *Short Line.* The back edge of the short line is midway between, and is parallel with, the front and back walls.

2. *Service Line.* The front edge of the service line is parallel with, and five feet in front of, the back edge of the short line.

3. *Service Zone.* The service zone is the five-foot area between the outer edges of the short line and service line.

4. *Service Boxes.* The service boxes are located at each end of the service zone and are designated by lines parallel with the side walls. The edge of the line nearest to the center of the court shall be 18 inches from the nearest side wall.

5. *Drive Serve Lines.* The drive serve lines, which form the drive serve zone, are parallel with the side wall and are within the service zone. The edge of the line nearest to the

center of the court shall be three feet from the nearest side wall.

6. *Receiving Line.* The receiving line is a broken line parallel to the short line. The back edge of the receiving line is five feet from the back edge of the short line. The receiving line begins with a line 21 inches long that extends from each side wall. These lines are connected by an alternate series of six-inch spaces and six-inch lines. This will result in a line composed of 17 six-inch spaces, 16 six-inch lines, and two 21-inch lines.

7. *Safety Zone.* The safety zone is the five-foot area bounded by the back edges of the short line and the receiving line. The zone is observed only during the serve. See Rules 4.11(k) and 4.12.

Rule 2.2 Ball Specifications

(a) The standard racquetball shall be 2 1/4 inches in diameter; weigh approximates 1.4 ounces; have a hardness of 55-60 inches durometer; and bounce 68-72 inches from a 100-inch drop at a temperature of 70-74 degrees Fahrenheit.

(b) Only a ball having the endorsement or approval of the AARA may be used in an AARA sanctioned tournament.

Rule 2.3 Ball Selection

(a) A ball shall be selected by the referee for use in each match. During the match the referee may, at his discretion or at the request of a player or team, replace the ball. Balls that are not round or which bounce erratically shall not be used.

(b) If possible, the referee and players should agree to an alternate ball, so that in the event of breakage, the second ball can be put into play immediately.

Rule 2.4 Racquet Specifications

(a) The racquet including bumper guard and all solid parts of the handle, may not exceed 21 inches in length.

(b) The racquet frame may be any material judged to be safe.

(c) The racquet frame must include a cord that must be securely attached to the players wrist.

(d) The string of the racquet should be gut, monofilament, nylon, graphite, plastic, metal, or a combination thereof, providing strings do not mark or deface the ball.

(e) Using an illegal racquet will result in forfeiture of the game in progress or, if discovered between games, forfeiture of the preceding game.

Rule 2.5 Apparel

(a) Effective September 1, 1995, lensed eyewear designed for racquetball, and which meets or exceeds ASTM F803 or Canadian (CSA) impact standards, is required apparel. This rule applies to all persons, including those who must wear corrective lenses. The eyewear must be worn as designed and at all times. A player who fails to wear proper eyewear will be assessed a technical foul and a timeout to obtain proper eyewear. A second infraction in the same match will result in immediate forfeiture of the match. (See Rule 4.18(a)9). The current AARA approved eyewear list is available from the AARAs national office.

(b) Clothing and Shoes. The clothing may be of any color; however, a player may be required to change wet, extremely loose fitting, or otherwise distracting garments. Insignias and writing on clothing must be considered to be in good taste by the tournament director. Shoes must have soles which do not mark or damage the floor.

(c) Equipment Requirement During Warm-up. Approved eyeguards must be worn and wrist cords must be used during any on-court warm-up period. The referee should give a technical warning to any person who fails to comply and assess a technical foul if that player continues to not comply after receiving such a warning.

3 - Officiating

Rule 3.1 Tournament Management

All AARA sanctioned tournaments shall be managed by a tournament director, who shall designate the officials.

Rule 3.2 Tournament Rules Committee

The tournament director may appoint a tournament rules committee to resolve any disputes that the referee, tournament desk, or tournament director cannot resolve. The committee, composed of an odd number of persons, may include state or national officials, or other qualified individuals in attendance who are prepared to meet on short notice. The tournament director should not be a member of this committee.

Rule 3.3 Referee Appointment and Removal

The principal official for every match shall be the referee who has been designated by the tournament director, or his designated representative, and who has been agreed upon by all participants in the match. The referee's authority regarding a match begins once the players are called to the court. The referee may be removed from a match upon the agreement of all participants (teams in doubles) or at the discretion of the tournament director or his designated representative. In the event that a referee's removal is requested by one player or team and not agreed to by the other, the tournament director or his designated representative may accept or reject the request. It is suggested that the match be observed before determining what, if any, action is to be taken. In addition, two line judges and a scorekeeper may also be designated to assist the referee in officiating the match.

Rule 3.4 Rules Briefing

Before all tournaments, all officials and players shall be briefed on rules as well as local court hinders, regulations, and modifications the tournament director wishes to impose. The briefing should be reduced to writing. The current AARA rules will apply and be made available. Any modifications the tournament director wishes to impose must be stated on the entry form and be available to all players at registration.

Rule 3.5 Referees

(a) Pre-Match Duties. Before each match begins, it shall be the duty of the referee to:

1. Check on adequacy of preparation of court with respect to cleanliness, lighting and temperature.

2. Check on availability and suitability of materials to include balls, towels, scorecard, pencils and timepiece necessary for the match.

3. Check the readiness and qualifications of the line judges and scorekeeper. Review appeal procedures and instruct them of their duties, rules and local regulations.

4. Go onto the court to introduce himself and the players; brief the players on court hinders, local regulations, rule modifications for this tournament; explain misinterpreted rules.

5. Inspect players equipment; identify the line judges; verify selection of a primary and alternate ball.

6. Toss coin and offer the winner the choice of serving or receiving.

(b) Decisions. During the match, the referee shall make all decisions with regard to the rules. Where line judges are used, the referee shall announce all final judgments. If both players in singles and three out of four in a doubles match disagree with a call made by the referee, the referee is overruled with the exception of technical fouls and forfeitures.

(c) Protests. Any decision not involving the judgement of the referee will, on protest, be accorded due process as set forth in the by-laws of the AARA. For the purposes of rendering a prompt decision regarding protests filed during the course of an ongoing tournament, the stages of due process will be first to the tournament director and second to the tournament rules committee. In those instances when time permits, the protest may be elevated to the state association and then to the National Board of directors in the manner prescribed in the by-laws.

(d) Forfeitures. A match maybe forfeited by the referee when:

1. Any player refuses to abide by the referee's decision or engages in unsportsmanlike conduct.

2. Any player or team who fails to report to play 10 minutes after the match has been scheduled to play. (The tournament director may permit a longer delay if circumstances warrant such a decision.)

(e) Defaults. A player or team may be forfeited by the tournament director or official for failure to comply with the tournament or host facility's rules while on the premises between matches, or for abuse of hospitality, locker room, or other rules and procedures.

(f) Spectators. The referee shall have jurisdiction over the spectators, as well as the players, while the match is in progress.

(g) Other Rulings. The referee may rule on all matters not covered in the AARA Official Rules. However, the referee's ruling is subject to protest as described in Rule 3.5 (c).

Rule 3.6 Line Judges

(a) When Utilized. Two line judges should be used for semifinal and final matches, when requested by a player or team, or when the referee or tournament director so desires. However, the use of line judges is subject to availability and the discretion of the tournament director.

(b) Replacing Line Judges. If any player objects to a person serving as a line judge before the match begins, all reasonable effort shall be made to find a replacement acceptable to the officials and players. If a player objects after the match begins, any replacement shall be at the discretion of the referee and/or tournament director.

(c) Position of Line Judges. The players and referee shall designate the court location of the line judges. Any dispute shall be settled by the tournament director.

(d) Duties and Responsibilities. Line judges are designated to help decide appealed calls. In the event of an appeal, and after a very brief explanation of the appeal by the referee, the line judges must indicate their opinion of the referee's call.

(e) Signals. Line judges should extend their arms and signal as follows: (i) thumb up to show agreement with the referee's call, (ii) thumb down to show disagreement, and (iii) hand open with palm facing down to indicate "no opinion" or that the play in question wasn't seen.

(f) Manner of Response. Line judges should be careful not to signal until the referee acknowledges the appeal and asks for a ruling. In responding to the referee's request, line judges should not look at each other, but indicate their opinion simultaneously in a clear view of the players and referee. If at any time a line judge is unsure of which call is being appealed or what the referee's call was the line judge should ask the referee to repeat the call and the appeal.

(g) Result of Response. If both line judges signal no opinion, the referee's call stands. If both line judges disagree with the referee, the referee must reverse the ruling. If one line judge agrees with the call and one disagrees, the referee's call stands. If one line judge agrees with the call and one has no opinion, the call stands. If one line judge disagrees with the referee's call and the other signals no opinion, the rally is replayed. Any replays, with the exception of appeals on the second serve itself, will result in two serves.

Rule 3.7 Appeals

(a) Appealable Calls and Non-Calls. In any match using line judges, a player may appeal only the following calls or noncalls by the referee: skip ball; fault serve, except screen serves; out serve; double bounce pickup; receiving line violation; and court hinder. At no time may a player appeal a screen serve, a hinder call (except court hinders), a technical foul, or other discretionary call of the referee.

(b) How to Appeal. A verbal appeal by a player must be made directly to the referee immediately after the rally has ended. A player who believes there is an infraction to appeal, should bring it to the attention of the referee and line judges by raising his non-racquet hand at the time the perceived infraction occurs. The player is obligated to continue to play until the rally has ended or the referee stops play. The referee will recognize a player's appeal only if it is made before that players leaves the court for any reason including timeouts and game-ending rallies or, if that player doesn't leave the court, before the next serve begins.

(c) Loss of Appeal. A player or team forfeits its right of appeal for that rally if the appeal is made directly to the line judges or, if the appeal is made after an excessive demonstration or complaint.

(d) Limit on Appeals. A player or team may make three appeals per game. However, if either line judge disagrees (thumb down) with the referees's call, that appeal will not count against the three-appeal limit. In addition, the game-ending rally may be appealed even if the three-appeal limit has been reached.

Rule 3.8 Outcome of Appeals

(a) Skip Ball. If the referee makes a call of "skip ball," the call may be appealed. If the call is reversed, the referee then must decide if the shot in question could have been returned had play continued. If in the opinion of the referee, the shot could have been returned, the rally shall be replayed. However, if the shot was not retrievable, the side which hit the shot in question is declared the winner of the rally. If the referee makes no call on a shot (thereby indicating that the shot did not skip), an appeal may be made that the shot skipped. If the no call is reversed, the side which hit the shot in question loses the rally.

(b) Fault Serve. If the referee makes a call of "fault serve," the call may be appealed. If the call is reversed, the serve is replayed, unless if the referee considered the serve to be not retrievable, in which case a point is awarded to the server. An appeal may also be made if the referee makes no call on a serve (indicating that the serve was good). If the no call is reversed, it will result in second serve if the infraction occurred on the first serve or loss of serve if the infraction occurred on the second serve.

(c) Out Serve. If the referee makes a call of "out serve," the call may be appealed. If the call is reversed, the serve will be replayed, unless the serve was obviously a fault in which case the call becomes fault serve. However, when the call is reversed and the serve is considered an ace, a point will be awarded. An appeal may also be made if the referee makes no call on a serve (indicating that the serve was good). If the no call is reversed, it results in an immediate loss of serve.

(d) Double Bounce Pickup. If the referee makes a call of "two bounces," the call may be appealed. If the call is reversed, the rally is replayed, except if the player against whom the call was made hit a shot that could not have been retrieved, then that player wins the rally. (Before awarding a rally in that situation, the referee must be certain that the shot would not have been retrieved even if play had not been halted.) An appeal may also be made if the referee makes no call thereby indicating that the get was not two bounces. If the no call is reversed, the player who made the two bounce pickup is declared the loser of the rally.

(e) Receiving Line Violation (Encroachment). If the referee makes a call of "encroachment," the call may be appealed. If the call is overturned, the service shall be replayed. An appeal may also be made if the referee makes no call. If the appeal is successful, the server is awarded a point.

(f) Court Hinder. If the referee makes a call of "court hinder," the rally is replayed. If the referee makes no call and a player feels that a court hinder occurred, that player may appeal. If the appeal is successful, the rally will be replayed.

Rule 3.9 Rules Interpretations

If a player feels the referee has interpreted the rules incorrectly, the player may require the referee or tournament director to show him the applicable rule in the rule book. Having discovered a misapplication or misinterpretation, the official must correct the error by replaying the rally, awarding the point, calling sideout or taking whatever corrective measure necessary.

4 - Play Regulations

Rule 4.1 Serve

The player or team winning the coin toss has the option to either serve or receive at the start of the first game. The second game will begin in reverse order of the first game. The player or team scoring the highest total of points in games 1 and 2 will have the option to serve or receive first at the start of the tiebreaker. In the event that both players or teams score an equal number of points in the first two games, another coin toss will take place and the winner of the toss will have the option to serve or receive.

Rule 4.2 Start

The server may not start the service motion until the referee has called the score or "second serve." The serve is started from any place within the service zone. Certain drive serves are an exception, see Rule 4.6. Neither the ball, nor any part of either foot may extend beyond either line of the service zone when initiating the service motion. Stepping on, but not over, the line is permitted. When completing the service motion, the server may step over the service (front) line provided that some part of both feet remain on or inside the line until the served ball passes, the short line. The server may not step over the short line until the ball passes the short line. See Rules 4.10 (a) and 4.11 (k) for penalties for violations.

Rule 4.3 Manner

After taking a set position inside the service zone, a player may begin the service motion—any continuous movement which results in the ball being served. Once the service motion begins, the ball must be bounced on the floor in the zone and be struck by the racquet before it bounces a second time. After being struck the ball must hit the front wall first and on the rebound hit the floor beyond the back edge of the short line, either with or without touching one of the side walls.

Rule 4.4 Readiness

The service motion shall not begin until the referee has called the score or the second serve and the server has visually checked the receiver. The referee shall call the score as both server and receiver prepare to return to their respective positions, shortly after the previous rally has ended.

Rule 4.5 Delays

Except as noted in Rule 4.5 (b), delays exceeding 10 seconds shall result in an out if the server is the offender or a point if the receiver is the offender.

(a) The 10 second rule is applicable to the server and receiver simultaneously. Collectively, they are allowed up to 10 seconds, after the score is called, to serve or be ready to receive. It is the server's responsibility to look and be certain the receiver is ready. If the receiver is not ready, he must signal so by raising his racquet above his head or completely turning his back to the server. (These are the only two acceptable signals.)

(b) Serving while the receiving player/team is signalling not ready is a fault serve.

(c) After the score is called, if the server looks at the receiver and the receiver is not signalling not ready, the server may then serve. If the receiver attempts to signal not ready after that point, the signal shall not be acknowledge and the serve becomes legal.

Rule 4.6 Drive and Service Zones

The drive serve lines will be 3 feet from each side wall in the service box, dividing the service area into two 17-foot service zones for drive serves only.

The player may drive serve between himself and the side wall nearest to where his service motion began only if the player starts and remains outside of the 3-foot drive serve zone. In the event that the service motion begins in one drive service zone and continues into the other drive serve zone, the player may not hit a drive serve at all. Violations of this rule, either called or not called, may be appealed.

(a) The drive serve zones are not observed for a cross court drive serves, the hard-Z, soft-Z, lob or half-lob serves.

(b) The racquet may not break the plane of the 17-foot zone while making contact with the ball.

(c) The drive serve line is not part of the 17-foot zone. Dropping the ball on the line or standing on the line while serving to the same side is an infraction.

Rule 4.7 Serve in Doubles

(a) Order of Serve. Each team shall inform the referee of the order of service which shall be followed throughout that game. The order of serve may be changed between games. At the beginning of each game, when the first server of the first team to serve is out, the team is out. Thereafter, both players on each team shall serve until the team receives a handout and a sideout.

(b) Partner's Position. On each serve, the server's partner shall stand erect with back to the side wall and with both feet on the floor within the service box from the moment the server begins the service motion until the served ball passes the short line. Violations are called foot faults. However, if the server's partner enters the safety zone before the ball passes the short line, the server loses service.

Rule 4.8 Defective Serves

Defective serves are of three types resulting in penalties as follows:

(a) Dead-Ball Serve. A dead-ball serve results in no penalty and the server is given another serve (without canceling a prior fault serve).

(b) Fault Serve. Two fault serves result in an out (either a sideout or a handout).

(c) Out Serve. An out serve results in an out (either a sideout or a handout).

Rule 4.9 Dead-ball Serves

Dead-ball serves do not cancel any previous fault serve. The following are dead-ball serves:

(a) Court Hinders. A serve that takes an irregular bounce because it hit a wet spot or an irregular surface on the court is a dead-ball serve. Also, any serve that hits any surface designated by local rules as an obstruction.

(b) Broken Ball. If the ball is determined to have broken on the serve, a new ball shall be substituted and the serve shall be replayed, not canceling any prior fault serve.

Rule 4.10 Fault Serves

The following serves are faults and any two in succession result in an out:

(a) Foot Faults. A foot fault results when:

1. The server does not begin the service motion with both feet in the service zone.

2. The server steps completely over the service line (no part of the foot on or inside the service zone) before the served ball crosses the short line.

3. In doubles, the server's partner is not in the service box with both feet on the floor and back to the side wall from the time the server begins the service motion until the ball passes the short line. See Rule 4.7 (b).

(b) Short Service. A short serve is any served ball that first hits the front wall and, on the rebound, hits the floor on or in front of the short line either with or without touching a side wall.

(c) Three Wall Serve. A three-wall serve is any served ball that first hits the front wall and, on the rebound, strikes both side walls before touching the floor.

(d) Ceiling Serve. A ceiling serve is any served ball that first hits the front wall and then touches the ceiling (with or without touching a side wall).

(e) Long Serve. A long serve is a served ball that first hits the front wall and rebounds to the back wall before touching the floor (with or without touching a side wall).

(f) Out-of-Court Serve. An out-of-court serve is any served ball that first hits the wall and, before striking the floor, goes out of the court.

(g) Bouncing Ball Outside Service Zone. Bouncing the ball outside the service zone as a part of the service motion is a fault serve.

(h) Illegal Drive Serve. A drive serve in which the player fails to observe the 17-foot drive service zone outlined in Rule 4.6.

(i) Screen Serve. A served ball that first hits the front wall and on the rebound passes so closely to the server, or server's partner in doubles, that it prevents the receiver from having a clear view of the ball. (The receiver is obligated to place himself in good court position, near center court, to obtain that view.) The screen serve is the only fault serve which may not be appealed.

(j) Serving Before the Receiver is Ready. A serve is made while the receiver is not ready as described in Rule 4.5.

(k) Ball Hits Partner. A served ball that hits the doubles partner while in the doubles box results in a fault serve.

Rule 4.11 Out Serves
Any of the following serves results in an out:

(a) Two consecutive Fault Serves. See Rule 4.10.

(b) Failure to Serve. Failure of server to put the ball into play under Rule 4.5.

(c) Missed Serve Attempt. Any attempt to strike the ball that results in a total miss or in the ball touching any part of the server's body.

Also, allowing the ball to bounce more than once during the service motion.

(d) Touched Serve. Any served ball that on the rebound from the front wall touches the server or server's racquet, or any ball intentionally stopped or caught by the server or server's partner.

(e) Fake or Balk Serve. Any movement of the racquet toward the ball during the serve which is noncontinuous and done for the purpose of deceiving the receiver. If a balk serve occurs, but the referee believes that no deceit was involved, he has the option of declaring "no serve" and have the serve replayed without penalty.

(f) Illegal Hit. An illegal hit includes contacting the ball twice, carrying the ball, or hitting the ball with the handle of the racquet or part of the body or uniform.

(g) Non-Front Wall Serve. Any served ball that does not strike the front wall first.

(h) Crotch Serve. Any served ball that hits the crotch of the front wall and floor, front wall and side wall, or front wall and ceiling is an out serve (because it did not hit the front wall first). A serve into the crotch of the back wall and floor is a good serve and in play. A served ball that hits the crotch of the side wall and floor beyond the short line is in play.

(i) Out-of-Order Serve. In doubles, when either partner serves out of order, the points scored by that server will be subtracted and an out serve will be called: if the second server serves out of order, the out serve will be applied to the first server and the second server will resume serving. If the player designated as the first server serves out of order, a sideout will be called. The referee should call no serve as soon as an out-of-order serve occurs. If no points are scored while the team is out of order, only the out penalty will have to be assessed. However, if points are scored before the out of order condition is noticed and the referee cannot recall the number, the referee may enlist the aid of the line judges (if they are being used) to recall the number of points to be deducted.

(j) Ball Hits Partner. A served ball that hits the doubles partner while outside the doubles box results in loss of serve.

(k) Safety Zone Violation. If the server, or doubles partner, enters into the safety zone before the served ball passes the short line, it shall result in the loss of serve.

Rule 4.12 Return of Service
(a) Receiving Position

1. The receiver may not enter the safety zone until the ball bounces or crosses the receiving line.

2. On the fly return attempt, the receiver may not strike the ball until the ball breaks the plane of the receiving line. The receiver's follow-through may carry the receiver or his racquet past the receiving line.

3. Neither the receiver nor his racquet may break the plane of the short line, except if the ball is struck after rebounding off the back wall.

4. Any violation by the receiver results in a point for the server.

(b) Defective Serve. A player on the receiving side may not intentionally catch or touch a served ball (such as an apparently long or short serve) until the referee has made a call or the ball has touched the floor for a second time. Violation results in a point.

(c) Legal Return. After a legal serve, a player on the receiving team must strike the ball on the fly or after the first bounce, and before the ball touches the floor the second time; and return the ball to the front wall, either directly or after touching one or both side walls, the back wall or the ceiling, or any combination of those surfaces. A returned ball must touch the front wall before touching the floor.

(d) Failure to return. The failure to return a serve results in a point for the server.

(e) Other Provisions. Except as noted in this rule (4.12), the return of serve is subject to all provisions of Rules 4.14 through 4.16.

Rule 4.13 Changes of Serve

(a) Outs. A server is entitled to continue serving until:

1. Out Serve. See Rule 4.11.

2. Two Consecutive Fault Serves. See Rule 4.10.

3. Ball Hits Partner. Player hits partner with attempted return.

4. Failure to Return Ball. Player, or partner, fails to keep the ball in play as required by Rule 4.12 (c).

5. Avoidable Hinder. Player or partner commits an avoidable hinder which results in an out. See Rule 4.16.

(b) Sideout. In singles, retiring the server is a sideout. In doubles, the side is retired when both partner's have lost service, except that the team which serves first at the beginning of each game loses the serve when the first server is retired. See Rule 4.7.

(c) Effect of Sideout. When the server (or serving team) receives a sideout the server becomes the receiver and the receiver becomes the server.

Rule 4.14 Rallies

All of the play which occurs after the successful return of serve is called the rally. Play shall be conducted according to the following rules:

(a) Legal Hits. Only the head of the racquet may be used at any time to return the ball. The racquet may be held in one or both hands. Switching hands to hit a ball, touching the ball with any part of the body or uniform, or removing the wrist thong results in a loss of the rally.

(b) One Touch. The player or team trying to return the ball may touch or strike the ball only once or else the rally is lost. The ball may not be carried. (A carried ball is one which rests on the racquet long enough that the effect is more of a sling or throw than a hit.)

(c) Failure to Return. Any of the following constitutes a failure to make a legal return during a rally:

1. The ball bounces on the floor more than once before being hit.

2. The ball does not reach the front wall on the fly.

3. The ball caroms off a player's racquet into a gallery or wall opening without first hitting the front wall.

4. A ball which obviously does not have the velocity or direction to hit the front wall strikes another player.

5. A ball struck by one player on a team hits that player or that player's partner.

6. Committing an avoidable hinder. See Rule 4.16.

7. Switching hands during a rally.

8. Failure to use wrist thong on racquet.

9. Touching the ball with the body or uniform.

10. Carry or sling the ball with the racquet.

(d) Effect of Failure to Return. Violations of Rules 4.14 (a)-(c) result in a loss of rally. If the serving player or team loses the rally, it is an out. If the receiver loses the rally, it results in a point for the server.

(e) Return Attempts. The ball remains in play until it touches the floor a second time, regardless of how many walls it makes contact with—including the front wall.

1. In singles, if a player swings at the ball and misses it, the player may continue to attempt to return the ball until it touches the floor for the second time.

2. In doubles, if one player swings at the ball and misses it, both partners may make further attempts to return the ball until it touches the floor the second time. Both partners on a side are entitled to return the ball.

(f) Out of Court Ball.
1. After return. Any ball returned to the front wall which, on the rebound or the first bounce, goes into the gallery or through an opening in a side wall shall be declared dead and the server shall receive two serves.

2. No Return. Any ball not returned to the front wall, but which caroms off a player's racquet into the gallery or into any opening in a side wall either with or without touching the ceiling, side wall, or back wall, shall be an out for the player failing to make the return, or a point for the opponent.

(g) Broken Ball. If there is any suspicion that a ball has broken during a rally, play shall continue until the end of the rally. The referee or any player may request that ball be examined. If the referee decides the ball is broken the ball will be replaced and the rally replayed. The server will get two serves. The only proper way to check a broken ball is to squeeze it by hand. (Checking the ball by striking it with a racquet will not be considered a valid check and shall work to the disadvantage of the player or team which struck the ball after the rally.)

(h) Play Stoppage.

1. If a foreign object enters the court, or any other outside interference occurs, the referee shall stop the play immediately and declare a dead-ball hinder.

2. If a player loses any apparel, equipment, or other article, the referee shall stop play immediately and declare an avoidable hinder or dead-ball hinder as described in Rule 4.16 (i).

(i) Replays. Whenever a rally is replayed for any reason, the server is awarded two serves. A previous fault serve is not considered.

Rule 4.15 Dead-ball Hinders
A rally is replayed without penalty and the server receives two serves whenever a dead-ball hinder occurs.

(a) Situations.
1. Court Hinders. The referee should stop play immediately whenever the ball hits any part of the court that was designated in advance as a court hinder (such as a door handle). The referee should also stop play (i) when the ball takes an irregular bounce as a result of contacting a rough surface

(such as court light or vent) or after striking a wet spot on the floor or wall and, (ii) when, in the referee's opinion, the irregular bounce affected the rally. A court hinder is the only type of hinder that is appealable. See Rule 3.7 (a).

2. Ball Hits Opponent. When an opponent is hit by a return shot in flight, it is a dead-ball hinder. If the opponent is struck by a ball which obviously did not have the velocity or direction to reach the front wall, it is not a hinder, and the player who hit the ball will lose the rally. A player who has been hit by the ball can stop play and make the call though the call must be made immediately and acknowledged by the referee.

3. Body Contact. If body contact occurs which the referee believes was sufficient to stop the rally, either for the purpose of preventing injury by further contact or because the contact prevented a player from being able to make a reasonable return, the referee shall call a hinder. Incidental body contact in which the offensive player clearly will have the advantage should not be called a hinder, unless the offensive player obviously stops play. Contact with the racquet on the follow-through normally is not considered a hinder.

4. Screen Ball. Any ball rebounding from the front wall so close to the body of the defensive team that it interferes with, or prevents, the offensive player from having clear view of the ball. (The referee should be careful not to make the screen call so quickly that it takes away a good offensive opportunity.) A ball that passes between the legs of the side that just returned the ball is not automatically a screen. It depends on the proximity of the players. Again, the call should work to the advantage of the offensive player.

5. Backswing Hinder. Any body or racquet contact, on the backswing or on the way to or just prior to returning the ball, which impairs the hitter's ability to take a reasonable swing. This call can be made by the player attempting the return, though the call must be made immediately and is subject to the referee's approval. Note the interference may be considered an avoidable hinder. See Rule 4.16.

6. Safety Holdup. Any player about to execute a return who believes he is likely to strike his opponent with the ball or racquet may immediately stop play and request a deadball

hinder. This call must be made immediately and is subject to acceptance and approval of the referee. (The referee will grant a dead-ball hinder if it is believed the holdup was reasonable and the player would have been able to return the shot and the referee may also call an avoidable hinder if warranted.)

7. Other Interference. Any other unintentional interference which prevents an opponent from having a fair chance to see or return the ball. Example: When a ball from another court enters the court during a rally or when a referee's call on an adjacent court obviously distracts a player.

(b) Effect of Hinders. The referee's call of hinder stops play and voids any situation which follows, such as the ball hitting the player. The only hinders that may be called by a player are described in rules (2), (5), and (6) above, and all of these are subject to the approval of the referee. A dead ball hinder stops play and the rally is replayed. The server receives two serves.

(c) Avoidance. While making an attempt to return the ball, a player is entitled to a fair chance to see and return the ball. It is the responsibility of the side that has just hit the ball to move so the receiving side may go straight to the ball and have an unobstructed view of the ball. In the judgment of the referee however, the receiver must make a reasonable effort to move towards the ball and have a reasonable chance to return the ball in order for a hinder to be called.

Rule 4.16 Avoidable Hinders
An avoidable hinder results in the loss of the rally. An avoidable hinder does not necessarily have to be an intentional act and is the result of any of the following:

(a) Failure to Move. A player does not move sufficiently to allow an opponent a shot straight to the front wall as well as a cross court shot which is a shot directly to the front wall at an angle that would cause the ball to rebound directly to the rear corner farthest from the player hitting the ball. Also, when a player moves in such a direction that it prevents an opponent from taking either of these shots.

(b) Stroke Interference. This occurs when a player moves, or fails to move, so that the opponent returning the ball does not have a free, unimpeded swing. This includes unintentionally moving the wrong direction which prevents an opponent from making an open offensive shot.

(c) Blocking. Moves into a position which blocks the opponent from getting to, or returning, the ball; or in doubles, a player moves in front of an opponent as the players' partner is returning the ball.

(d) Moving into the Ball. Moves in the way and is struck by the ball just played by the opponent.

(e) Pushing. Deliberately pushes or shoves opponent during a rally.

(f) Intentional Distractions. Deliberate shouting, stamping of feet, waving of racquet, or any manner of disturbing one's opponent.

(g) View Obstruction. A player moves across an opponent's line of vision just before the opponent strikes the ball.

(h) Wetting the Ball. The players, particularly the server, should insure that the ball is dry prior to the serve. Any wet ball that is not corrected prior to the serve shall result in an avoidable hinder against the server.

(i) Apparel or Equipment Loss. If a player loses any apparel, equipment, or other article, play shall be immediately stopped and that player shall be called for an avoidable hinder, unless the player has just hit a shot that could not be retrieved. If the loss of equipment is caused by a player's opponent, then a dead-ball hinder should be called. If the opponent's action is judged to have been avoidable, then the opponent should be called for an avoidable hinder.

Rule 4.17 Timeouts

(a) Rest Periods. Each player or team is entitled to three 30-second timeouts in games to 15 and two 30-second timeouts in games to 11. Timeouts may not be called by either side after service motion has begun. Calling for a timeout when none remain or after service motion has begun, or taking more than 30 seconds in a timeout, will result in the assessment of a technical foul for delay of game.

(b) Injury. If a player is injured during the course of a match as a result of contact, such as with the ball, racquet, wall or floor, he will be awarded an injury timeout. While a player may call more than one timeout for the same injury or for additional injuries which occur during the match, a player is not allowed more than a total of 15 minutes of rest during a match. If the injured player is not able to resume play after total rest of 15 minutes, the match shall be awarded to the opponent. Muscle cramps and pulls, fatigue, and other ailments that are not caused by direct contact on the court will not be considered an injury.

(c) Equipment Timeouts. Players are expected to keep all clothing and equipment in good, playable condition and are expected to use regular timeouts and time between games for adjustment and replace-ment of equipment. If a player or team is out of timeouts and the referee determines that an equipment change or adjustment is necessary for fair and safe continuation of the match, the referee may award an equipment timeout not to exceed 2 minutes. The referee may allow additional time under unusual circumstances.

(d) Between Games. The rest period between the first two games of a match is 2 minutes. If a tiebreaker is necessary, the rest period between the second and third game is 5 minutes.

(e) Postponed Games. Any games postponed by referees shall be resumed with the same score as when postponed.

Rule 4.18 Technical Fouls and Warnings

(a) Technical Fouls. The referee is empowered to deduct one point from a player's or team 's score when, in the referee's sole judgment, the player is being overtly and deliberately abusive. If the player or team against whom the technical foul was assessed does not resume play immediately, the referee is empowered to forfeit the match in favor of the opponent. Some examples of actions which may result in technical fouls are:

1. Profanity.
2. Excessive arguing.
3. Threat of any nature to opponent or referee.
4. Excessive or hard striking of the ball between rallies.
5. Slamming of the racquet against walls or floor, slamming the door, or any action which might result in injury to the court or other players.
6. Delay of game. Examples include (i) taking too much time to dry the court, (ii) questioning of the referee excessively about the rules, (iii) exceeding the time allotted for timeouts or between games, or (iv) calling a timeout when none remain.
7. Intentional front line foot fault to negate a bad lob serve.
8. Anything considered to be unsportsmanlike behavior.
9. Failure to wear lensed eyewear designed for racquet sports is an automatic technical foul on the first infraction and a mandatory timeout will be charged against the offending player to acquire the proper eyewear. A second infraction by that player during the match will result in automatic forfeiture of the match.

(b) Technical Warnings. If a player's behavior is not so severe as to warrant a technical foul, a technical warning may be issued without point deduction.

(c) Effect of Technical Foul or Warning. If a referee issues a technical foul, one point shall be removed from the offender's score. If a referee issues a technical warning, it shall not result in a loss of rally or point and shall be accompanied by a brief explanation of the reason for the warning. The issuing of the technical foul or warning has no effect on who will be serving when play resumes. If a technical foul occurs between games or when the offender has no points, the result will be that the offenders score will revert to minus one (-1).

5 - Tournaments

Rule 5.1 Draws

(a) If possible, all draws shall be made at least 2 days before the tournament commences. The seeding method of drawing shall be approved by the AARA.

(b) At AARA National events, the draw and seeding committee shall be chaired by the AARA's Executive Director, National Tournament Director, and the host tournament director. No other persons shall participate in the draw or seeding unless at the invitation of the draw and seeding committee.

(c) In local and regional tournaments the draw shall be the responsibility of the tournament director.

Rule 5.2 Scheduling

(a) Preliminary Matches. If one or more contestants are entered in both singles and doubles, they may be required to play both singles and doubles on the same day or night with little rest between matches. This is a risk assumed on entering two singles events or a singles and doubles event. If possible, the schedule should provide at least 1 hour between matches.

(b) Final Matches. Where one or more players has reached the finals in both singles and doubles, it is recommended that the doubles match be played on the day preceding the singles. This would assure more rest between on the final matches. If both final matches must be played on the same day or night, the following procedure is recommended that:

1. The singles match be played first.

2. A rest period of not less than 1 hour be allowed between the finals in singles and doubles.

Rule 5.3 Notice of Matches

After the first round of matches, it is the responsibility of each player to check the posted schedules to determine the time and place of each subsequent match. If any change is made in the schedule after posting, it shall be the duty of the committee or tournament director to notify the players of the change.

Rule 5.4 Third Place

Players are not required to play off for third place. However, for points standings, if one semifinalist wants to play off for third and the other semifinalist does not, the one willing to play shall be awarded third place. If neither semifinalist wishes to play off for third then the points shall be totaled, divided by 2 and awarded evenly to both players.

Rule 5.5 Round Robin Scoring

The final positions of players or teams in round robin competition is determined by the following sequence:

a. Winner of the most matches;

b. In a two-way tie, winner of the head-to-head match;

c. In a tie of three or more, the player who lost the fewest games is awarded the highest position.

(1) If a two-way tie remains, the winner of the head-to-head match is awarded the higher position.

(2) If a multiple tie remains, the total points scored against each player in all matches will be tabulated and the player who had the least points scored against him is awarded the highest position. Note: Forfeits will count as a match won in two games. In cases where points scored against is the tiebreaker, the points scored by the forfeiting team will be discounted from consideration of points scored against all teams.

Rule 5.6 Tournament Management

In all AARA sanctioned tournaments, the tournament director and/or AARA official in attendance may decide on a change of court after the completion of any tournament game, if such a change will accommo-date better spectator conditions.

Rule 5.7 Tournament Conduct

In all AARA sanctioned tournaments, the referee is empowered to forfeit a match, if the conduct of a player or team is considered detri-mental to the tournament and the game. See Rules 3.5 (d) and (e).

Rule 5.8 Professional

A professional is defined as any player who has accepted prize money regardless of the amount in any professional sanctioned (including

WPRA and IRT) tournament or in any other tournament so deemed by the AARA Board of Directors. (Note: Any player concerned about the adverse effect of losing amateur status should contact the AARA National Office at the earliest opportunity to ensure a clear understanding of this rule and that no action is taken that could jeopardize that status.)

(a) An amateur player may participate in a professional sanctioned tournament but will not be considered a professional (i) if no prize money is accepted or (ii) if the prize money received remains intact and placed in trust under AARA guidelines.

(b) The acceptance of merchandise or travel expenses shall not be considered prize money, and thus does not jeopardize a player's amateur status.

Rule 5.9 Return to Amateur Status

Any player who has been classified as a professional can recover amateur status by requesting, in writing, this desire to be reclassified as an amateur. This application shall be tendered to the Executive Director of the AARA or his designated representative, and shall become effective immediately as long as the player making application for reinstatement of amateur status has received no money in any tournament, as defined in Rule 5.8 for the past 12 months.

Rule 5.10 AARA Eligibility

(a) Any current AARA member who has not been classified as a professional (See Rule 5.8) may compete in any AARA sanctioned tournament.

(b) Any current AARA member who has been classified as a professional may compete in any event at on AARA sanctioned tournament that offers prize money or merchandise.

Rule 5.11 Divisions

(a) Open Division. Any player with amateur status.

(b) Adult Age Division. Eligibility is determined by the player's age on the first day of the tournament. Division are:

19+ - Junior Veterans	55+ - Golden Masters
25+ - Junior Veterans	60+ - Veteran Golden Masters
30+ - Veterans	65+ - Senior Golden Masters
35+ - Seniors 40+	70+ - Advanced Golden Masters
40+ - Veteran Seniors	75+ - Super Golden Masters
45+ - Masters	80+ - Grand Masters
50+ - Veteran Masters	

(c) Junior Age Divisions. Player eligibility is determined by the player's age on January 1st of current calendar year. Division are:

18 & under	10 & under
16 & under	8 & under
14 & under	8 & under multi-bounce
12 & under	

Rule 5.12 Division Competition by Gender

Men and women may compete only in events and divisions for their respective gender during regional and national tournaments. If there is not sufficient number of players to warrant play in a specific division, the tournament director may place the entrants in a comparably competitive division. Note: For the purpose of encouraging the development of women's racquetball, the governing bodies of numerous states permit women to play in men's divisions when a comparable skill level is not available in the women's divisions.

Rule 5.13 AARA Regional Championships

(a) Adult Regional Tournaments

1. Regional tournaments will be conducted at various metro sites designated annually by the AARA and players may compete at any site they choose.

2. A person may compete in any number of adult regional tournaments, but may not enter a championship (no skill designation) division after having won that division at a previous adult regional tournament that same year.

3. A person cannot participate in more than two championship events at a regional tournament.

4. Any awards or remuneration to an AARA National Championship will be posted on the entry blank.

(b) Junior Regional Tournaments. All provisions of Rule 5.13 (a) also apply to juniors except:

1. Regional tournaments will be conducted within the following regions which are identified for the purposes of junior competition:

Region	1	Maine, N.H., VT., Mass., R.I, Conn.
Region	2	New York, New Jersey
Region	3	PA., Maryland, Virginia, Delaware, D. C.
Region	4	Florida, Georgia
Region	5	Alabama, Mississippi, Tennessee
Region	6	Arkansas, Kanas, Missouri, Oklahoma
Region	7	Texas, Louisiana

Region	8	Wisconsin, Iowa, Illinois
Region	9	West Virginia, Ohio, Michigan
Region	10	Indiana, Kentucky
Region	11	N.D., S.D., Minn., Neb.
Region	12	Arizona, New Mexico, Utah, Colorado
Region	13	Montana, Wyoming
Region	14	California, Hawaii, Nevada
Region	15	Washington, Idaho, Oregon, Alaska
Region	16	North Carolina, South Carolina

2. A person may compete in only one junior regional singles and one junior regional doubles tournament each year.

3. Rule 5.13 (a)(3) may not apply if tournaments (singles/doubles or adults/juniors) are combined.

Rule 5.14 U.S. National Singles Championships and U.S. National Doubles Championships

The U.S. National Singles and Doubles Tournaments are separate tournaments and are played on different dates. Consolation events will be offered for all divisions.

(a) Competition in an adult regional singles tournament is required to qualify for the National Singles Championship. Current National Champions are exempt from qualifying for the next year's championships.

(b) The National Tournament Director may handle the rating of each region and determine how many players shall qualify from each regional tournament.

(c) If a region is over subscribed, a playoff to qualify players in a division may be conducted the day prior to the start of a National Championship.

Rule 5.15 U.S. National Junior Olympic Championships

It will be conducted on a different date than all other National Championships and generally subject to the provisions of Rule 5.14.

Rule 5.16 U.S. National High School Championships

It will be conducted on a different date than all other National Championships. Consolation events will be offered for all divisions.

Rule 5.17 U.S. National Intercollegiate Championships

It will be conducted on a different date than all other National Championships. Consolation events will be offered for all divisions.

Rule 5.18 U.S. National Skill Level (A,B,C,D) Championships

It will be conducted on a different date than all other National Championships. Consolation events will be offered for all divisions.

6 - Eight and Under Multi-bounce

In general, the AARA's standard rules governing racquetball play will be followed except for the modifications which follow.

Rule 6.1 Basic Return Rule

In general, the ball remains in play as long as it is bouncing. However, the player may swing only once at the ball and the ball is considered dead at the point it stops bouncing and begins to roll. Also, anytime the ball rebounds off the back wall, it must be struck before it crosses the short line on the way to the front wall, except as explained in Rule 6.2.

Rule 6.2 Blast Rule

If the ball caroms from the front wall to the back wall on the fly, the player may hit the ball from any place on the court— including past the short line— so long as the ball is bouncing.

Rule 6.3 Front Wall Lines

Two parallel lines (tape may be used) should be placed across the front wall such that the bottom edge of one line is 3 feet above the floor and the bottom edge of the other line is 1 foot above the floor. During the rally, any ball that hits the front wall (i) below the 3-foot line and (ii) either on or above the 1-foot line must be returned before it bounces a third time. However, if the ball hits below the 1-foot line, it must be returned before it bounces twice. If the ball hits on or above the 3-foot line, the ball must be returned as described in the basic return rule.

Rule 6.4 Games and Matches

All games are played to 11 points and the first side to win two games, wins the match.

7 - One-wall and Three-wall

In general, the AARA's standard rules governing racquetball play will be followed except for the modifications which follow.

Rule 7.1 One-wall

There are two playing surfaces the front wall and the floor. The wall is 20 feet wide and 16 feet high. The floor is 20 feet wide and 34 feet to the back edge of the long line. To permit movement by players, there should be a minimum of three feet (six feet is recommended) beyond the long line and six feet outside each side line.

(a) Short Line. The back edge of the short line is 16 feet from the wall.

(b) Service Markers. Lines at least six inches long which are parallel with, and midway between, the long and short lines. The extension of the service markers from the imaginary boundary of the service line.

(c) Service Zone. The entire floor area inside and including the short line, side lines and service line.

(d) Receiving Zone. The entire floor area in back of the short line, including the side lines and the long line.

Rule 7.2 Three-wall with Short Side Wall
The front wall is 20 feet wide and 20 feet high. The side walls are 20 feet long and 20 feet high, with the side walls tapering to 12 feet high. The floor length and court markings are the same as a four wall court.

Rule 7.3 Three-wall with Long Side Wall
The court is 20 feet wide, 20 feet high and 40 feet long. The side walls may taper from 20 feet high at the front wall down to 12 feet high at the end of the court. All court markings are the same as a four wall court.

Rule 7.4 Service in Three-wall Courts
A serve that goes beyond the side walls on the fly is an out. A serve that goes beyond the long line on a fly, but within the side walls, is a fault.

8 - Wheelchair (NWRA)

Rule 8.1 Changes to Standard Rules
In general, the AARA's standard rules governing racquetball play will be followed except for the National Wheelchair Racquetball Association [NWRA] modifications which follow.

(a) Where AARA rules refer to server, person, body, or other similar variations, for wheelchair play such reference shall include all parts of the wheelchair in addition to the person sitting on it.

(b) Where the rules refer to feet standing or other similar descriptions, for wheelchair play it means only where the rear wheels actually touch the floor.

(c) Where the rules mention body contact, for wheelchair play it shall mean any part of the wheelchair in addition to the player.

(d) Where the rules refer to double bounce or after the first bounce, it shall mean three bounces. All variations of the same phrases shall be revised accordingly.

Rule 8.2 Divisions
(a) Novice Division. The novice division is for the beginning player who is just learning to play.

(b) Intermediate Division. The Intermediate Division is for the player who has played tournaments before and has a skill level to be competitive in the division.

(c) Open Division. The Open Division is the highest level of play and is for the advanced player.

(d) Multi-Bounce Division. The Multi-Bounce Division is for the individuals (men or women) whose mobility is such that wheelchair racquetball would be impossible if not for the Multi-Bounce Division.

(e) Junior Division. The junior divisions are for players who are under the age of 19. The tournament director will determine if the divisions will be played as two bounce or multi-bounce. Age divisions are: 8-11, 12-15, and 16-18.

Rule 8.3 Rules

(a) Two Bounce Rule. Two bounces are used in wheelchair racquetball in all divisions except the Multi-Bounce Division. The ball may hit the floor twice before being returned.

(b) Out-of-Chair Rule. The player can neither intentionally jump out of his chair to hit a ball nor stand up in his chair to serve the ball. If the referee determines that the chair was left intentionally it will result in loss of the rally for the offender. If a player unintentionally leaves his chair, no penalty will be assessed. Repeat offenders will be warned by the referee.

(c) Equipment Standards. In order to protect playing surfaces, the tournament officials may not allow a person to participate with black tires or anything that will mark or damage the court.

(d) Start. The serve may be started from any place within the service zone. Although the front casters may extend beyond the lines of the service zone, at no time shall the rear wheels cross either the service or short line before the served ball crosses the short line. Penalties for violation are the same as those for the standard game.

(e) Maintenance Delay. A maintenance delay is a delay in the progress of a match due to a malfunction of a wheelchair, prosthesis, or assistive device. Such delay must be requested by the player, granted by the referee during the match, and shall not exceed 5 minutes. Only two such delays may be granted for each player for each match. After using both maintenance delays, the player has the following options: 1. Continue play with the defective equipment. 2. Immediately substitute replacement equipment. 3. Postpone the game, with the approval of the referee and opponent.

Rule 8.4 Multi-bounce Rules

(a) The ball may bounce as many times as the receiver wants though the player may swing only once to return the ball to the front wall.

(b) The ball must be hit before it crosses the short line on its way back to the front wall.

(c) The receiver cannot cross the short line after the ball contacts the back wall.

9 - Visually Impaired

In general, the AARA's standard rules governing racquetball play will be followed except for the modifications which follow.

Rule 9.1 Eligibility

A player's visual acuity must not be better than 20/200 with the best practical eye correction or else the player's field of vision must not be better than 20 degrees. The three classification of blindness are B1 (totally blind to light perception), B2 (able to see hand movement up to 20/600 corrected), and B3 (from 20/600 to 20/200 corrected).

Rule 9.2 Return of Serve and Rallies

On the return of serve and on every return thereafter, the player may make multiple attempts to strike the ball until (i) the ball has been touched, (ii) the ball has stopped bouncing, or (iii) the ball has passed the short line after touching the back wall. The only exception is described in Rule 9.3.

Rule 9.3 Blast Rule

If the ball (other than on the serve) caroms from the front wall to the back wall on the fly, the player may retrieve the ball from any place on the court - including in front of the short line—so long as the ball has not been touched and is still bouncing.

Rule 9.4 Hinders

A dead-ball hinder will result in the rally being replayed without penalty unless the hinder was intentional. If a hinder is clearly intentional, an avoidable hinder should be called and the rally awarded to the nonoffending player or team.

10 - Hearing Impaired (NRAD)

In general, the AARA's standard rules governing racquetball play will be followed except for the National Racquetball Association of the Deaf modifications which follow.

Rule 10.1 Eligibility

An athlete shall have a hearing loss of 55 db or more in the better ear to be eligible for any NRAD tournament.

11 - Women's Professional Racquetball Association (WPRA)

In general, the AARA's standard rules governing racquetball play will be followed for competition on the Women's Professional Racquetball

Association tour, except for the modifications which follow:

Rule 11.1 Match, Game, Super Tiebreaker
A match is won by the first side winning three games. All games, other than the fifth one, are won by the first side to score 11 points. The fifth game, called the super tiebreaker, is won by the first side scoring 11 points and having at least a 2-point lead. If necessary, the game will continue beyond 11 points until such time as one side has a 2-point lead.

Rule 11.2 Appeals
There is no limit on the number of appeals that a player or team may make.

Rule 11.3 Serve
The server may leave the service zone as soon as the serve has been made.

Rule 11.4 Drive Service Zone
The server may begin a drive serve anywhere in the service zone so long as the server is completely inside the 17-foot drive service zone when the ball is actually contacted.

Rule 11.5 Return of Serve
The receiver may enter the safety zone as soon as the ball has been served. The served ball may not be contacted in the receiving zone until it has bounced. Neither the receiver nor the receiver's racquet may break the plane of the short line unless the ball is struck after rebounding off the back wall. On the fly return attempt, the receiver may not strike the ball until the ball breaks the plane of the receiving line. The receiver's follow through may carry the receiver or the racquet past the receiving line.

Rule 11.6 Avoidable Hinder
An avoidable hinder shall be called when one of the following occurs:

(a) The player's movement or failure to move interferes with their opponents's opportunity to take an offensive shot. The player is entitled to a free, unimpeded swing on their shot. The player should not be blocked by the opponent, preventing their getting to or returning the ball for an offensive shot.

(b) Any other action or conduct described in Rules 4.16 (d) through 4.16 (i).

Rule 11.7 Timeouts
Each player or team is entitled to two 30-second timeouts per game.

Rule 11.8 Time Between Games
The rest period between all games will be 2 minutes except that a 5-minute rest period will be allowed between the fourth and fifth games.

Rule 11.9 Equipment Timeouts
A player does not have to use regular timeouts to correct or adjust equipment provided that the need for the change or adjustment is acknowledged by the referee as being necessary for fair and safe continuation of the match.

12 - International Racquetball Tour
[IRT/Men's Professional]
In general, the AARA's standard rules governing racquetball play will be followed for competition in the Transcoastal International Racquetball Tour, except for the modifications which follow:

Rule 12.1 Game, Match
All games are played to 11 points, and are won by the player who scores to that level, with a 2-point lead. If necessary, the game will continue beyond 11 points, until such time as one player has a 2-point lead. Matches are played the best three out of a possible five games to 11.

Rule 12.2 Appeals
The referee's call is final. There are no line judges, and no appeals may be made.

Rule 12.3 Serve
Players are allowed only one serve to put the ball into play.

Rule 12.4 Screen Serve
Screen serves are replayed.

Rule 12.5 Court Hinders
No court hinders are allowed or called.

Rule 12.6 Out of Court Ball
Any ball leaving the court results in a loss of rally.

Rule 12.7 Ball
All matches are played with the Penn Pro ball.

Rule 12.8 Timeouts
Each player is entitled to one 1-minute timeout per game.

Rule 12.9 Time Between Games
The rest period between all games is 2 minutes.

Rule Change Procedures

To ensure the orderly growth of racquetball, the AARA has established specific procedures that are followed before a major change is made to the rules of the game. Those procedures are:

1. Rule change proposals must be submitted in writing to the AARA National Office by June 1st.

2. The AARA Board of Directors will review all proposals at its October board meeting and determine which will be considered.

3. Selected proposals will appear in *Racquetball* Magazine— the official AARA publication—as soon as possible after the October meeting for comment by the general membership.

4. After reviewing membership input and the recommendation of the National Rules Committee and National Rules Commissioner, the proposals are discussed and voted upon at the annual Board of Directors meeting in May.

5. Changes approved in May become effective on September 1st. Exception: changes in racquet specifications become effective 2 years later on September 1st.

6. Proposed rules that are considered for adoption in one year, but are not approved by the Board of Directors in May of that year, will not be considered for adoption the following year.

This complete set of official rules was reprinted with permission of the AARA, which governs the game.

Language of the Game

ace: A serve untouched by the receiver.

avoidable hinder: Interference that could have been prevented that results in automatic loss of the rally.

back court: The back third of the court nearest the back wall.

backhand: Hitting the ball from the side opposite the forehand.

backswing: Taking the racquet back in preparation for beginning the swing.

blocking: Preventing opponent from hitting ball by moving some part of body between opponent and ball.

ceiling shot: A shot hit off the ceiling-front wall-floor before bounding in a high arc to deep rear court.

court: The playing area.

crotch ball: A ball hitting at the junction of the floor and a wall.

cut-off: A form of volley.

cut-throat: A game involving three players with each player in his or her turn as server playing against the other two.

dead ball: A ball no longer in play.

doubles: Two players playing against two other players.

drive: Hitting the ball low and forcefully to the front wall so that it rebounds relatively parallel to the floor.

drive serve zone: Two areas located near either end of the service zone marked with a line parallel to and three feet away from both side walls.

drop shot: A shot hit softly contacting the front wall low and near the corner to minimize the rebound.

error: Failure to successfully return a playable ball hit during the rally.

exchange: The rally or continuous alternating shots between opponents.

fault: An infraction of the service rule.

follow-through: The continuation of the swing of the racquet after the ball has been hit.

foot fault: Illegal position of one or both of the server's feet during the serve.

fly shot: A shot in flight before it bounces once; cut-off shot; volley.

forehand: Hitting the ball on the dominant-hand side or opposite side of the backhand.

front court: The court area in front of the service line.

garbage serve: A short lob serve which first contacts the floor near the short line.

half volley: Hitting the ball immediately after it bounces from the floor.

hinder: Unintentional interference with an opponent during play resulting in replay of point.

illegal serve: Failure to serve the ball in accordance with the playing rules.

kill: A ball hit so low to the front wall that it is practically unplayable.

lead foot: The foot positioned nearer the front wall when in the striking position.

lob: A ball hit gently to a targeted spot high on the front wall so that it rebounds in a high arc to deep or short back court.

mask: Creating an outward appearance to conceal the intended shot.

match: The best two out of three games.

pass: A ball hit to the side and out of the reach of an opponent.

pinch shot: A kill shot that is directed low off either side wall near the corner which rebounds into the front wall.

placement: Hitting the ball to an intended position on the court.

racquet face: Strung striking area of the racquet frame.

rally: The playing time of opponents between the serve and the end of the point; the exchange.

receiver: The non-server(s).

receiving line: A broken line parallel to and located 5 feet behind the short line.

rest period: Intervals during and between games in accordance with the rules.

screen: Interference with opponent's vision in attempting to play the ball.

serve: The act of hitting the ball from within the service zone to begin play.

server: The player who initiates the rally.

service box: In doubles, the area in which the server's partner must remain until the serve has passed the short line.

service line: A line parallel to and five feet in front of the short line.

service zone: The area between and including the service line and the short line.

serve-out: A player losing serve in accordance with the rules.

shadow serve: A served ball passing so close to the server's body on the rebound that the receiver is unable to pick up the flight of the ball.

short: A serve failing to contact the floor beyond the short line.

short line: A line midway between and parallel to the front and back walls.

sideout: Loss of service by a player in singles or both players in doubles.

singles: One player against one other player.

sliding: A combination of a step and a run in which the lead step is quickly followed by a closing of the free foot to replace the supporting foot.

sweet spot: Hitting surface in the top center of the racquet head which provides the most power and control.

throat: The part of the racquet between the strings and the grip.

volley: Hitting the ball in the air on the rebound off any wall or the ceiling before it bounces; fly shot.

wrist thong: A loop of small rope attached to the end of the racquet handle which is worn around the wrist for safety.

Z-ball: A defensive shot that contacts the front wall near the corner, bounds off the side wall and bounces off the floor into the opposite side wall.

Chapter 8

1. The game of racquetball may be played by two, three, or four players. What are the terms describing each of these versions of the game?

2. What is the specific term for loss of serve for both the singles and the doubles versions of the games?

3. In a match in which the opponents, in the first two games, each win a game, a third and deciding game must be played. What is the third game called?

4. What total score is required to win the first two games in a match and how does the third deciding game "winning score" differ?

5. The rules list the dimensions of the court as 20 feet by 40 feet by 20 feet. Which of these three figures represent the length, width and height of the court? What do the rules convey about the height of the back wall of the court?

6. There are two floor markings (lines) that enclose a five-foot area named the "service zone." What are the markings (lines) called in the published rules of the game and what is their relative location to each other in terms of the front wall?

7. Name the areas located at each end of the service zone enclosed by a line eighteen inches from and parallel to the side walls.

8. Name the broken line and the area of the court enclosed by the short line and the side walls.

9. What is the regulation on racquet length?

10. What do the rules dictate with regards to lensed eyeware and wrist cords during on-court warm-up periods in tournament play?

Chapter 8, *continued*

11. As it relates to serving or receiving the serve, what determines which player or team serves or receives in the second game? What is the player or team option, as it relates to serving or receiving, in a required third and deciding game?

12. The serve can begin from any position within the service zone but neither the ball, nor any part of either foot may extend beyond either line that defines the service zone. What is the rule concerning the player stepping on either line while serving?

13. There are regulations concerning the service motion, once started and the manner the ball is bounced prior to it being served. What are those two regulations?

14. What is the responsibility of the server, prior to serving the ball, to the receiver in singles play or receivers in doubles play?

15. What is the purpose of the drive serve zone areas defined by a three foot line from either side wall? Name a drive serve where the drive serve zones rule is not observed?

16. In doubles play the rules specify that the order of the serve, once determined, shall be followed throughout a game. With that in mind, while playing the same match, can the order of the serve be changed between games? What is the rule on the first serve of each game in doubles?

17. Name the area in doubles that the non-serving partner must occupy during the serve? According to the rules, what stance is the partner of the server to assume in the designated area during the serve?

Chapter 8, *continued*

18. Name three types of defective serves that result in a penalty.

19. Identify the following examples of dead-ball serves.

    a. The serve hits a wet spot on the floor, an irregular surface on the court or a surface designated by local rules as an obstruction.

    b. The ball breaks on the serve.

20. Any two fault serves in succession result in an out.

    a. Describe two actions of the server and one by the doubles partner in the box that result in a fault serve.

    b. For a serve to be labeled a short service, where on the floor, relative to the service zone, must the ball bound, after hitting the front wall with or without hitting the side wall?

    c. What do the following fault serves have in common, besides the fact each hits the front wall first: three-wall serve, ceiling serve, long serve, and the out-of-court serve?

d. Name the serve that bounds directly off the front wall and passes closely by the server preventing the receiver of the serve, in the singles or doubles play, from having a clear view.

21. Name the following out serves.

   a. A total miss of the ball, or, the ball, while being bounced, touches any part of the servers body.

   b. The ball, upon rebounding from the front wall, contacts the server or the server's racquet, or, any ball intentionally stopped or caught by the server or the server's partner.

   c. Purposeful deception on the part of the server through faking a serve.

   d. Contacting the ball twice or hitting the ball with the handle of the racquet or part of the body or uniform.

   e. Any serve that does not contact the front wall first.

   f. Any served ball that hits the juncture of the front wall and floor; front wall and side wall; or front wall and ceiling.

   g. When either server in a doubles match serve out of the established order.

   h. A ball that hits a partner of the server outside the doubles box.

   i. If the server, or a doubles partner, enters into the safety zone before the served ball passes the short line.

Chapter 8, *continued*

22. There are three violations by a receiver of the serve that result in a point for the server. These involve the service zone, the receiving line and the short line. What are the restrictions placed on the receiver as it relates to each of these?

23. What constitutes a legal return by the receiver?

24. Does the term "sideout," in retiring the server (or servers) apply to singles play, doubles play, or both?

25. Name the term used to describe continued play after there is a successful return of the serve?

26. The rules stipulate that the racquet can be held by one or two hands during play. What do the rules specify about switching hands to strike the ball or removing the wrist thong?

27. Define the term "carrying the ball," an illegal touch of the ball which is considered as a failure to return the ball, as stated in the rules.

28. "Avoidable hinder" is a term repeated throughout the rules. In your own words, what constitutes an avoidable hinder?

29. Is there a limit to the number of walls a ball may contact, including the front wall, prior to bounding on the floor before it is is considered out of play?

30. What do the rules specify in the case of a missed swing by a singles or a doubles player?

31. What is the out of court ball rule as it relates to a player who strikes the ball which travels directly into the gallery as opposed to a player who strikes the ball which contacts the front wall and then bounds directly into the spectators gallery?

32. Give examples of dead-ball hinders—circumstances that cause play to be stopped by a referee or a player.

Chapter 8, *continued*

33. One dead-ball hinder rule entitled "avoidance" states that a player is entitled to a fair chance to see and return the ball. What does this rule mean to the player or side (in doubles) that just hit the ball?

34. Avoidable hinders include a number of acts by opponents that result in the loss of the rally. Name the following avoidable hinders?

    a. A player does not move sufficiently to allow an opponent a shot.

    b. A player does not move sufficiently to allow the opponent a free unimpeded swing.

    c. A player moves into a position which impedes an opponent from getting to, or returning the ball.

    d. A player moves into the path of the ball and is struck with the ball.

    e. A player delibertly contacts and shoves an opponent during a rally.

    f. A player exhibits disruptive behavior.

    g. A player moves across an opponent's line of vision just before the opponent strikes the ball.

    h. A player, as the server, fails to dry the ball prior to serving.

35. There are specific rules for each of the situations that allow for timeouts. What are the three types of timeouts listed in the rules?

Selected References

Allsen, Phillip E., and Pete Witbeck. *Racquetball*. Dubuque, Iowa: William C. Brown Publishers, 1988.

Isaacs, Larry D., Angela Lumpkin, and Don Schroer. *Racquetball Everyone*. Winston-Salem, North Carolina: Hunter Textbooks Incorporated, 1984.

Kozar, Andrew J., Rodney J. Grambeau, and Earl N. Riskey. *Beginning Paddleball*. Belmont, California: Wadsworth Publishing Company, Incorporated, 1969.

McKay, Heather. *Heather McKay's Complete Book of Squash*. New York, New York: Ballantine Books, 1979.

Plotnicki, Ben A., and Andrew J. Kozar. *Handball*. Dubuque, Iowa: Kendal/Hunt Publishing Company, 1970.

Spear, Victor I. *Sports Illustrated Racquetball*. Chicago, Illinois: Time Incorporated, 1979.

Verner, Bill. *Racquetball: Basic Skills and Drills*. Palo Alto, California: Mayfield Publishing Company, 1985.

Wright, Shannon, and Steve Keeley. *The Women's Book of Racquetball*. Chicago, Illinois: Contemporary Books Incorporated, 1980.